# The Management of
# Wage Payment Systems

# The Management of Wage Payment Systems

Alan Gillespie

Kogan Page (Associates)

First published 1973 by
Kogan Page (Associates) Limited
116a Pentonville Road, London N1 9JN

Setting by Dahling Dahling, London

Printed in Great Britain by
Compton Printing Ltd., Aylesbury

SBN 85038 240 8

# Payment Systems

Payment systems vary according to the nature and organisation of the work, local conditions and other factors, but the following principles apply generally.

Payment systems should be:
  (i) kept as simple as possible, consistent with their purpose, so that employees can understand them:
  (ii) based on some form of work measurement where payment is linked to performance:
  (iii) jointly negotiated where trade unions are recognised.

Difference in remuneration should be related to the requirements of the job, which should wherever possible be assessed in a rational and systematic way in consultation with employee representatives.

Payment systems should be kept under review to make sure that they suit current circumstances and take account of any substantial changes in the organisation of work or the requirements of the job.

*Code of Practice with the authority*
*of Parliament under the*
*Industrial Relations Act 1971 S3(1)*

# Contents

# Preface

Although one name appears on the cover of this work I would like to express my gratitude to all those who assisted in its preparation, my colleagues at the Manchester Business School and in particular Professor Tom Lupton, Dan Gowler and Karen Legge. The work would not have been possible but for the co-operation I received from members of the following firms, some of whom contributed by discussing the ideas of the book, others by exemplifying their use and to these I am also grateful:

British Leyland Limited
P.J. Carroll Limited
Cummins Limited
Delta Metals Limited
Ferodo Limited
Honeywell Limited
Laurence Scott Limited
Pilkington Brothers Limited
Victory Kidder Limited

Several other firms co-operated but wished to remain anonymous. Finally, I would like to thank the Engineering Employers' Federation for the provision of support for this work, and to express my gratitude to Mrs. V. Vose and Mrs. M. Dickson who typed the preliminary and final drafts.

Alan Gillespie
Manchester Business School
September 1971

# 1    Introduction

In 1969 Tom Lupton and Dan Gowler published *Selecting a Wage Payment System*. The Engineering Employers' Federation, which sponsored and published the work, also sponsored the present work to discover whether the procedure devised by Lupton and Gowler was as useful a practical tool for management diagnosis and decision as it appeared. I was asked to carry out the investigation; this book is the outcome. The first part of the book reproduces and explains their ideas and procedures.

Lupton and Gowler argue that the experience of generations of managers has shown that there are many different ways of relating effort and reward and many different kinds of effort and reward depending on what is being produced, by what processes, and by what kind of workers. There are many different kinds of payment systems; payment-by-results schemes of various kinds, systems that link time-related inducements to performance criteria, individual and group plans, bonus schemes related to plant output as a whole and so on. Some payment systems are observed to work well in some situations but not in others. They observe a natural tendency amongst managers not to seek reasons for success and to attribute failure to one or two obvious factors. They think it unsatisfactory that managers' experiences with payment systems were not assembled in a systematic way to indicate which payment systems were appropriate for which situations, and in the light of what objectives.

They point to some of the factors that have to be taken into account in choosing an appropriate payment system — product markets, labour markets, technology, trade unions, and the attitudes and expectations of workpeople. Of course there are further factors that must be considered by the manager making decisions about modifying or changing a payment system. All these factors are present in every situation; every manufacturing company has customers and competitors, plant and machinery, procedures for organizing them to complete a task, and workpeople with attitudes and expectations; but the factors differ in their effects from situation to situation and from time to time in any one situation. They recognise that to assemble systematically research findings and the experience of management about payment systems, they needed a method of measuring differences in these factors: hence they could say with some accuracy how the technology of one company differs from the technology of another, or from one period of time to another in the recent history and projected future of the same firm; how the conditions in the labour market and the product market may be accurately compared, and so on.

To systemize the experience of management requires a method of classifying payment schemes in such a way that they may be matched to the circumstances as defined. Although there have been attempts to classify payment systems the criteria for classification have not been designed especially to assist in selecting a payment system, nor in such a way as to make possible the design of novel payment systems especially designed to match unprecedented or unusual circumstances.

They explain later in greater detail what might seem at this stage to be a neglect of worker motivation though it is true that they concentrate on what may be called structural factors defined as those factors external to the individual that influence his behaviour. It could be argued that different individuals might react in different ways to the same external influence, or that all individuals will try to shape their environment to give expression to their needs for interesting work, congenial company, scope to exercise personal judgement, and the desire to participate in decisions which affect their jobs; and that all individual human beings have similar needs to satisfy. It has been said that when certain basic needs are satisfied, e.g. for food, clothing, shelter, then higher order needs call for satisfaction such as the need for work which allows self-expression and involves recognition of one's personal contribution. All of this Lupton and Gowler accept. They expect that management might provide opportunities for self-expression, which would be to re-define jobs so as to enlarge the range of skill and judgement required, and therefore the training needed, within the limits the technology imposes. The increased job interest which might be promised as a result could be regarded as an inducement to the individual to join the organisation and to perform well in response to the system relating effort and reward. Similarly, arrangements for worker participation in decision making might be regarded as an inducement to join, and stay to perform well.

They deal with all these matters; firstly, by classifying payment schemes so as to take into account workers' motivations; secondly, by including in the method of defining a situation an opportunity to provide for them in the design of the organization and thirdly by including in them the possible objectives that managers might set for themselves. They do not deal with them by considering what payment system will move an individual to high performance, given the characteristics of that individual. Rather, they take the view that the behaviour of individuals which is what we are interested in, can only sensibly be considered in relation to the particular circumstances in which they are placed (indeed motives can only be deduced from observations of behaviour in situ). The basic question that they tackle throughout their work is: what combination of organization, environment and payment system is best fitted to satisfy a given set of objectives?

So for all its apparently complex structure, the Lupton-Gowler procedure claims to expose (though more rigorously and completely) the reasoning underlying practical managers' decisions about payment systems. They argue that decisions about payment systems usually involve four elements —

1. A set of aims defining what a payment system ought to do (e.g. maximise productivity, minimise labour turnover).

13

2. An idea about how many different systems of payment there are to choose from, and the characteristics of each.
3. A knowledge of the set of circumstances of which the payment system is a part.
4. A procedure for deciding which of the various systems available will best match the circumstances of the case, given the aims.

It is easy to see how the aims of management might be frustrated, if their knowledge of payment systems, or their ability to define the circumstances relevant to particular systems, is faulty or incomplete. Lupton and Gowler drew upon their own research and that of others, to construct an exhaustive logical classification of payment systems, to define and measure the variables relevant to the operation of payment systems, and to draw from the classification the alternative(s) best suited to a particular (quantified) set of circumstances. The aims and objectives of management, whatever they may be, can be made an integral part of the procedure.

The research reported here simply took the Lupton-Gowler procedure and used it as a framework to diagnose the payment systems of a number of firms. The results were used as a basis for discussion with managers in the firm, on whether they thought that the procedure accurately pointed out all the short-comings, and provided plausible reasons why changes of certain kinds ought to be made, i.e. whether it made sense to, and heightened the understanding of, practising managers with long experience of payment systems. In one sense, therefore, this book is a small collection of detailed case examples, analysed within a common framework, making possible useful comparisons of experience. Most of the areas of firms analysed were identified by management as a 'payment problem' — and consequently the emphasis is on the weaknesses of methods of payment in particular situations. The procedure was used to assess these actual problems. In many of the firms using the procedure, decisions were made to change the method of payment, to alter the situation, or to change the associated supervisory and staff organisation. On the whole the procedure made a significant contribution to diagnosis of the payment areas analysed either on its own or in conjunction with other methods used.

However, just as important, the practical application has been a 'de-bugging' exercise for the procedure. It has raised questions about the nature of the classification of payment systems, problems of definition and measurement of the profile dimensions, the matching procedure, and finally other problems to do with the implementation of change. This enables refinements to be made to the method.

The plan of work is simple. Firstly, I give a summary of the various elements of the procedure for selecting a payment system and give an example of its use. In the next section material from the firms studied is analysed and commented upon. Finally the findings of the survey are discussed.

# 2     The Procedure Explained

A detailed account of the procedure which is only outlined here is contained in the original version of *Selecting a Wage Payment System,* by Lupton and Gowler[1]. The procedure includes:

1. a method of classifying payment systems
2. a method of profiling the situation of a firm or part of a firm
3. a means of matching the situation to the appropriate method of payment
4. a concluding evaluation and change procedure.

The work could be described as a 'rationalistic' attempt to tease out the relevant experience of managers, researchers and consultants in order to formulate a systematic procedure for examining the complex problem of evaluating payment systems. However, the authors do not deny that managers also have objectives, values and assumptions and that these should or do in fact play a part in the selection of methods of payment. This is substantially evidenced in the description and analysis of payment systems that was undertaken in part three. Lupton and Gowler do not ignore these managerial assumptions or preferences in their procedure and make it possible to take account of such factors in what they refer to as 'profile analysis' to obtain 'value preferred' or 'modified' profiles. Indeed, they recommend that before using the method, managers might find it useful to make their objectives, values and assumptions as explicit as possible so that:

[1] Published by Kogan Page Ltd.

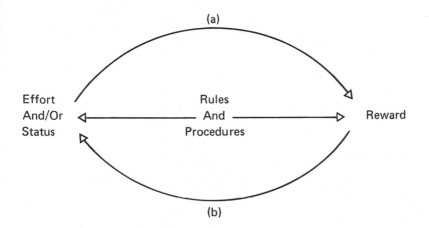

**Main Logical Types Of Payment Systems**

**Reciprocal immediate:**   rules and procedures immediate, reward is dependent on effort (b) and effort is dependent on reward (a).

**Reciprocal deferred:**   rules and procedures deferred, as above, though the relationship between (a) and (b) operates over a period of time.

**Non-reciprocal:**   rules and procedures non-reciprocal, no relationship between (a) and (b) via fixed pay rules.

*Figure 1. Diagrammatic Representation Of Payment Systems*

a) these might be taken account of in the procedure; and
b) that they might evaluate the consequences of holding such objectives, values and assumptions in their current or future situation.

Such explicitly stated values and assumptions about behaviour might refer to the significance of the 'cash incentive', 'job satisfaction' or 'staff status', as being the basis for improved labour productivity, or refer to some conviction that conditions are different today and hence methods of payments need to take account of such changed conditions, whereas others might hold that conditions have not changed significantly, and past practice in payment is still appropriate. When it comes to management's objectives these might be as diverse as, and might include, improving the consistency of labour performances, reducing labour turnover, improving product delivery dates, improving cost forecasts, reducing stock levels, improving consultative procedures and so on. Lupton and Gowler argue that these *all* have implications for the method of payment and the appropriateness of the method of payment, and consequently form part of their procedure[2].

They define payment systems in terms of the sets of rules and procedures that relate some kind of effort to some kind of reward, and in such terms they then identify several types of effort, reward and effort-reward relationships (i.e. sets of rules and procedures). Figure 1 illustrated these three main aspects of payment systems and each main type of payment system is characterised as having differing types of 'feedback loops' between reward and effort. These are the different rules and procedures of payment systems. The main types of such rules and procedures are identified as *reciprocal immediate, reciprocal deferred* and *non-reciprocal*. *Reciprocal immediate* rules state that the reward for effort is immediately forthcoming. *Reciprocal deferred* rules relating reward and effort are those where the reward is deferred. Finally, *non-reciprocal* rules are those where there is no feedback, i.e. no fixed rules that relate reward and effort;

[2]Op Cit. p. 30-35 and p. 8-10

18

here for example, the reward structure is usually fixed.

They then state that these basic types of effort and reward relationships are in practice the basis of different types of methods of payment; for example, 'reciprocal immediate' — incentive bonus schemes, 'reciprocal deferred' — some productivity bonus schemes, and 'non-reciprocal' — some measured day work schemes. In conjunction with these types of effort and reward relationships, and the different types of effort and types of reward they formulate a grid of payment schemes based on these characteristics.

The Logical Classification of Payment Systems (Figure 2)

| | | | Reward | | |
|---|---|---|---|---|---|
| | | | Reciprocal | | Non Reciprocal |
| | | | Immediate | Deferred | |
| Effort | | Time | TRI | TRD | TNR |
| | Energy | Individual | ERI (Ind) | ERD (Ind) | ENR (Ind) |
| | | Group | ERI (Group) | ERD (Group) | ENR (Group) |
| | | Competence | CRI | CRD | CNR |
| | | Status | X | X | SNR |

Figure 2. The Logical Grid Of Payment Systems

attempts to represent all possible types of reward, effort and effort-reward relationships. In practice many so-called 'incentive' or 'piecework' schemes are not reciprocal immediate in the manner defined by Lupton and Gowler, i.e., they may not in fact relate reward and effort in a particular situation. *Lupton and Gowler are primarily concerned to classify and analyse payment systems in terms of these basic mechanisms of rules and procedures that relate reward and effort rather than make use of piecemeal definitions which do not deal with the full range of payment systems.* To demonstrate the usefulness of this classification they then classify the commonly known payment methods in terms of the principles of the logical classification grid (Figure 3). In this manner they illustrate the range of alternatives that exist and the main differences in design between the different payment methods. For further detail the reader should refer to the book where the authors deal in detail with the basis of the classification and describe the main types of payment schemes.[3]

A combination of types of methods of payment might then be appropriate to any one firm. This, of course, is usually the case in many firms though the particular combination of types and the proportion of the labour force paid by the different methods of payment varies from firm to firm. Many managements 'inherit' the method or methods by which they pay their labour force. Some firms regard it as a *given* aspect of the firm, i.e. the suitability of the current method or methods of payment is not evaluated nor alternative methods sought. The firm's management unquestionably assumes the utility of their traditional method or methods of payment. It might in fact be well suited to the firm's circumstances and objectives and consequently facilitate the achievement of the firm's objectives. However, circumstances might well change and the rules and procedures of the traditional method of payment might well thwart the firm's objectives. Management might then seek improvement or change if they recognise the inadequacies of their method of payment.

[3] Op cit. p.16-20 and 45-53

| | | TRI | TRD | TNR |
|---|---|---|---|---|
| Time | | **TRI**<br>Time rates, with reciprocal payments, e.g. shift-and over-time premiums | **TRD**<br>Time rates, with reciprocal payments (or their equiva-lents) deferred, e.g. day off in lieu | **TNR**<br>Pay hour by hour for the hour |
| Energy | Individual | **ERI** (Ind)<br>Piecework Incentive bonus schemes Simple multi-factor schemes Price lists | **ERD** (Ind)<br>Individual productivity bonus Personal contract schemes | **ENR** (Ind)<br>Task work Measured day work Controlled day work |
| Energy | Group | **ERI** (GP)<br>Group piecework Group incentive bonus schemes Group simple multi-factor schemes Price lists | **ERD** (GP)<br>Group productivity bonus Scanlon and Rucker type schemes Profit sharing | **ENR** (GP)<br>Contract work |
| Competence | | **CRI**<br>Complex multi-factor schemes schemes based on analytical estimating | **CRD**<br>Work simplification Incremental scales with 'bars' based on performance | **CNR**<br>Full incremental salary scales Professional fees |
| Status | | X | X | **SNR**<br>Fringe benefits Ascription rewards |

*Figure 3. Payment System Classification*

To represent the firm's current circumstances Lupton and Gowler construct a 'profile' (Figure 4). This includes indicating the type of 'effort' and 'accountability' of the *current* method of payment in the 'gates' of the profile i.e. 1(g) and 2(g) in Figure 4. *The 'gates' are not related to the subsequent scales or scores as are the other profile dimensions.* The rest of the profile consists of a number of *related* dimensions each *one* representing an aspect of a typical production unit. These dimensions have been identified as being influential to the effectiveness of payment systems; each *one* is scaled, and each represent characteristics of technology, labour market, disputes and dispute procedures, as well as certain features of the organisation structure of the firm or part of the firm that is analysed.

The 'situation profile' is completed by scoring on each scaled dimension for the particular situation that is being examined. The configuration of profile scores represents the 'profile pattern' of the situation. A full analysis of a firm might then require the construction of profiles for each major area of the firm. The authors stress that the choice of the dimensions and the scales adopted were based on informed professional judgement and incomplete factual evidence from research and consultancy.[4]

Having completed the scores on the 'profile' measures, the next step is to translate these measurements to R.I., R.D. and N.R. scores (i.e. reciprocal immediate, reciprocal deferred and non-reciprocal scores). The crude numerical weighting given to the R.I. R.D. and N.R. scores represent the authors assessment (based on their experience) of the relative importance of these factors. This then provides a starting point for more careful examination. It should be apparent that the authors neither universally condemn or support any *one* particular method of payment but consider that certain payment methods are better suited to certain situations. The 'Payment Systems Master Block' (Figure 5) is an attempt to relate the situations's dimensional scores with the R.I., R.D., and N.R. scores (i.e. the different types of effort-reward

---

[4] Op. Cit. pp. 11-15 and 43-54. The notes on scoring the profile dimensions occur on pp 24-29, but to assist the reader these are also reproduced in an appendix at the end of this book.

| | Time | | | Energy | | | Competence | | | |
|---|---|---|---|---|---|---|---|---|---|---|
| | Individual | | | Group | | | Plant | | | |
| | 1 | 2 | 3 | 4 | 5 | 6 | 7 | 8 | 9 | |
| Length of job cycle | to 5 | 6-10 | 11-15 | 16-30 | 31-45 | 46-60 | 61-90 | 91-120 | 121+ | Mins. |
| Number of job modifications | 0 | 1 | 2 | 3 | 4 | 5 | 6 | 7 | 8+ | Av. no. per month |
| Degree of automation | SPT | PAT | SMT | CMT | STM | CTM | SPO | CPO | CCP | |
| Number of product changes | 0 | 1 | 2 | 3 | 4 | 5 | 6 | 7 | 8+ | Av. no. per month |
| Number of job stoppages | 0 | 1 | 2 | 3 | 4 | 5 | 6 | 7 | 8+ | Av. no. per day |
| Duration of job stoppages | 0 | 1-5 | 6-10 | 11-20 | 21-30 | 31-40 | 41-50 | 51-60 | 61+ | Av. no. mins. per day |
| % job elements specified by management | 71+ | 61-70 | 51-60 | 41-50 | 31-40 | 21-30 | 11-20 | 1-10 | 0 | % |
| % material scrapped | 0 | 1-2 | 3-4 | 5-6 | 7-8 | 9-10 | 11-12 | 13-14 | 15+ | % |
| % products/components rejected | 0 | 1-2 | 3-4 | 5-6 | 7-8 | 9-10 | 11-12 | 13-14 | 15+ | % |
| Time required to fill vacancy | 1 | 2-4 | 5-7 | 8-10 | 11-13 | 14-16 | 17-19 | 20-22 | 23+ | Days |
| Labour stability | 81+ | 71-80 | 61-70 | 51-60 | 41-50 | 31-40 | 21-30 | 11-20 | 0-10 | % |
| Labour turnover | 0 / 0 | 6 / 12 | 12 / 24 | 18 / 36 | 24 / 48 | 30 / 60 | 36 / 72 | 42 / 84 | 48 / 96 | Men % Women % |
| Disputes about pay | 0-4 | 5-8 | 9-12 | 13-16 | 17-20 | 21-24 | 25-28 | 29-32 | 33+ | Av. no. per month |
| Man hours lost in pay disputes | 0-4 | 5-8 | 9-12 | 13-16 | 17-20 | 21-24 | 25-28 | 29-32 | 33+ | % per month |
| % earnings decided outside plant/company | 0-10 | 11-20 | 21-30 | 31-40 | 41-50 | 51-60 | 61-70 | 71-80 | 81+ | % |
| Number of trade unions | 0 | 1-3 | 4-6 | 7-9 | 10-12 | 13-15 | 16-18 | 19-21 | 22+ | All plant |
| Occupational structure | 0-3 | 4-6 | 7-9 | 10-12 | 13-15 | 16-18 | 19-21 | 22-24 | 25+ | All plant |
| Absence | 0 | 2-3 | 4-5 | 6-7 | 8-9 | 10-11 | 12-13 | 14-15 | 16+ | % normal hours |
| Average age of working force | 15-29 | | | 30-44 | | | 45+ | | | Years |
| % labour cost in unit cost | 23+ | 21-23 | 18-20 | 15-17 | 12-14 | 10-12 | 7-9 | 4-6 | 1-3 | % |
| % males in working force | 0 | to 10 | 11-20 | 21-30 | 31-40 | 41-50 | 51-60 | 61-70 | 71+ | % All plant |

*Figure 4. Profile*

23

| 1(g) Type of effort | Time | | | Energy | | | Competence | | |
|---|---|---|---|---|---|---|---|---|---|
| 2(g) Unit of accountability | Individual | | | Group | | | Plant | | |
| | 1 | 2 | 3 | 4 | 5 | 6 | 7 | 8 | 9 | |

| | | | | | | | | | | | |
|---|---|---|---|---|---|---|---|---|---|---|---|
| | | 3RI | 2RI | 1RI | 3RD | 2RD | 1RD | 1NR | 2NR | 3NR | |
| 1 | Length of job cycle | to 5 | 6-10 | 11-15 | 16-30 | 31-45 | 46-60 | 61-90 | 91-120 | 121+ | Mins. |
| | | 3RI | 2RI | 1RI | 3RD | 2RD | 1RD | 1NR | 2NR | 3NR | |
| 2 | Number of job modifications | 0 | 1 | 2 | 3 | 4 | 5 | 6 | 7 | 8+ | Av. no. per month |
| | | 3RI | 2RI | 1RI | 3RD | 2RD | 1RD | 1NR | 2NR | 3NR | |
| 3 | Degree of automation | SPT | PAT | SMT | CMT | ŞTM | CTM | SPO | CPO | CCP | |
| | | 3RI | 2RI | 1RI | 3RD | 2RD | 1RD | 1NR | 2NR | 3NR | |
| 4 | Number of product changes | 0 | 1 | 2 | 3 | 4 | 5 | 6 | 7 | 8+ | Av. no. per month |
| | | 3RI | 2RI | 1RI | 3RD | 2RD | 1RD | 1NR | 2NR | 3NR | |
| 5 | Number of job stoppages | 0 | 1 | 2 | 3 | 4 | 5 | 6 | 7 | 8+ | Av. no. per day |
| | | 3RI | 2RI | 1RI | 3RD | 2RD | 1RD | 1NR | 2NR | 3NR | |
| 6 | Duration of job stoppages | 0 | 1-5 | 6-10 | 11-20 | 21-30 | 31-40 | 41-50 | 51-60 | 61+ | Av. no. min. per day |
| | | 3RI | 2RI | 1RI | 3RD | 2RD | 1RD | 1NR | 2NR | 3NR | |
| 7 | % job elements specified by management | 71+ | 61-70 | 51-60 | 41-50 | 31-40 | 21-30 | 11-20 | 1-10 | 0 | % |
| | | 3RI | 2RI | 1RI | 3RD | 2RD | 1RD | 1NR | 2NR | 3NR | |
| 8 | % material scrapped | 0 | 1-2 | 3-4 | 5-6 | 7-8 | 9-10 | 11-12 | 13-14 | 15+ | % |
| | | 3RI | 2RI | 1RI | 3RD | 2RD | 1RD | 1NR | 2NR | 3NR | |
| 9 | % products/components rejected | 0 | 1-2 | 3-4 | 5-6 | 7-8 | 9-10 | 11-12 | 13-14 | 15+ | % |
| | | 3RI | 2RI | 1RI | 3RD | 2RD | 1RD | 1NR | 2NR | 3NR | |
| 10 | Time required to fill vacancy | 1 | 2-4 | 5-7 | 8-10 | 11-13 | 14-16 | 17-19 | 20-22 | 23+ | Days |
| | | 3RI | 2RI | 1RI | 3RD | 2RD | 1RD | 1NR | 2NR | 3NR | |
| 11 | Labour stability | 81+ | 71-80 | 61-70 | 51-60 | 41-50 | 31-40 | 21-30 | 11-20 | to 10 | % |
| | | 3RI | 2RI | 1RI | 3RD | 2RD | 1RD | 1NR | 2NR | 3NR | |
| 12 | Labour turnover | 0 | 6 | 12 | 18 | 24 | 30 | 36 | 42 | 48 | Men % |
| | | 0 | 12 | 24 | 36 | 48 | 60 | 72 | 84 | 96 | Women % |
| | | 3RI | 2RI | 1RI | 3RD | 2RD | 1RD | 1NR | 2NR | 3NR | |
| 13 | Disputes about pay | 0-4 | 5-8 | 9-12 | 13-16 | 17-20 | 21-24 | 25-28 | 29-32 | 33+ | Av. no. per month |
| | | 3RI | 2RI | 1RI | 3RD | 2RD | 1RD | 1NR | 2NR | 3NR | |
| 14 | Man hours lost in pay disputes | 0-4 | 5-8 | 9-12 | 13-16 | 17-20 | 21-24 | 25-28 | 29-32 | 33+ | % per month |
| | | 3RI | 2RI | 1RI | 3RD | 2RD | 1RD | 1NR | 2NR | 3NR | |
| 15 | % earnings decided outside plant/company | 0-10 | 11-20 | 21-30 | 31-40 | 41-50 | 51-60 | 61-70 | 71-80 | 81+ | % |
| | | 3RI | 2RI | 1RI | 3RD | 2RD | 1RD | 1NR | 2NR | 3NR | |
| 16 | Number of trade unions | 0 | 1-3 | 4-6 | 7-9 | 10-12 | 13-15 | 16-18 | 19-21 | 22+ | All plant |
| | | 3RI | 2RI | 1RI | 3RD | 2RD | 1RD | 1NR | 2NR | 3NR | |
| 17 | Occupational structure | 0-3 | 4-6 | 7-9 | 10-12 | 13-15 | 16-18 | 19-21 | 22-24 | 25+ | All plant |
| | | 3RI | 2RI | 1RI | 3RD | 2RD | 1RD | 1NR | 2NR | 3NR | |
| 18 | Absence | 0 | 2-3 | 4-5 | 6-7 | 8-9 | 10-11 | 12-13 | 14-15 | 16+ | % normal hours |
| | | 3RI | | | 3RD | | | 3NR | | | |
| 19 | Average age of working force | 15-29 | | | 30-44 | | | 45+ | | | Years |
| | | 3RI | 2RI | 1RI | 3RD | 2RD | 1RD | 1NR | 2NR | 3NR | |
| 20 | % labour cost in unit cost | 23+ | 21-23 | 18-20 | 15-17 | 12-14 | 10-12 | 7-9 | 4-6 | 1-3 | % |
| | | 3RI | 2RI | 1RI | 3RD | 2RD | 1RD | 1NR | 2NR | 3NR | |
| 21 | % males in working force | 0 | to 10 | 11-20 | 21-30 | 31-40 | 41-50 | 51-60 | 61-70 | 71+ | % All plant |

*Figure 5. Payment Systems Master Block*

24

relationships). This 'matching' procedure then related the types of payment systems (the alternatives of which are represented in the logical classification of payment systems) with the different types of situations (which are represented by the profile scores obtained for a situation). From the 'Master Block' one reads off the R.I., R.D., and N.R. scores from the recorded dimensions of the situation. One then has an indication of the appropriateness of the method or methods of payment for the profiled situation. The authors refer to this as the idea of 'fit' between the method of payment and the situation. The effort-reward relation established by a payment method in a particular situation is then the outcome of the 'fit' and 'misfit' dimensions. This is usually represented by the structure of the pay packet for a particular situation[5]. The type of payment method determines the basic 'logicai' pay packet structure though over a period of time the actual resultant pay packet structure would be shaped by the impact of the particular mix of R.I., R.D. and N.R. scores which might influence the growth or contraction of parts of the pay packet; for example, pressures to adjust basic rates, or provide other forms of 'extra payment' or 'allowances'. All such dimensional factors would influence the method of payment as a source of motivation for the operators. Similarly, under certain payment methods management and supervision would be motivated to minimise or adjust to the impact of 'misfit' dimensions to maintain the effort-reward relationship by, for example, re-organising the work, changing stock levels, improving production scheduling, adjusting supervisory style, or adjusting quality standards and so on. The score on each dimension then indicates the appropriateness of that particular situational characteristic to a given payment method — an indication of the 'fit' of payment method and situation. The completed profile represents the mix of 'fit' and 'misfit' dimensions for a particular payment method. The

[5] For a lucid mathematical approach to the design of a pay packet structure see Angela Bowey and Tom Lupton *Productivity Drift and the Structure of the Pay Packet The Journal of Management Studies Vol. 7, No. 2, May 1970 (Part I) and Vol. 7, No. 3, October, 1970 (Part II).*

appropriateness of this 'fit' of the payment method then has implications for productivity improvement within a firm.

The final step is an overall evaluation procedure[6] which is used to assess the cost-saving potentiality and difficulty of changing the situation. These two aspects of any situation are evaluated on the 'Potentiality — Difficulty Grid' (Figure 6). This places the appropriateness of the payment system and the possibility of improvement in the context of the costs and constraints of the situation. It is suggested that managers should rank those aspects of the situation that are identified as being important on these two basic dimensions. This exercise might focus on the significant 'misfit' profile dimensions or be used to assess the current effect of certain working arrangements, practices, environmental constraints or managerial objectives. In this manner some overall strategy might be developed that takes account of current and future changes in the firm's objectives and circumstances. Strengths and weaknesses might be clearly revealed and substantial benefits might come from changing a few dimensions. It was not always possible during the application of the method (as described) to undertake the full and detailed evaluation procedure represented by the Potentiality — Difficulty Grid though often the evidence raised by the diagnostic assessment was sufficient not to require this final step.

These are then the main elements of the procedure:

    (a) the classification of payment systems
    (b) the profiling procedure
    (c) the means of matching profile and payment method and
    (d) the potentiality — difficulty grid.

As a guide to the steps one might take using the procedure, Lupton and Gowler detail the steps in selecting a wage payment system on page 35. However, it is not expected that the user rigidly adheres to the sequence or necessarily includes all of the steps in every analysis that is undertaken.

[6] Op. cit. pp. 30-32

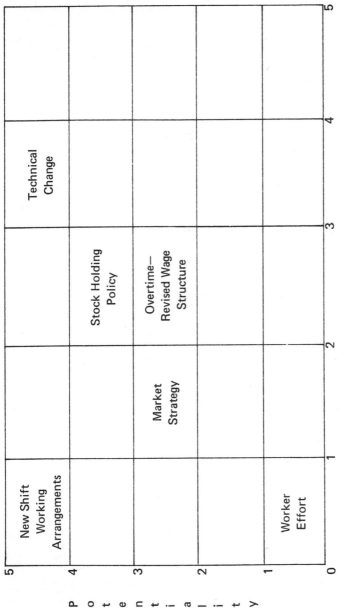

*Figure 6. Potentiality—Difficulty Grid*

27

The user might well focus on those aspects of the procedure that are most important to their firm.

The book sets out to answer in some detail whether

(a) the Lupton-Gowler method is a better way of selecting or improving a wage payment system than the methods employed by the firms that were investigated.
(b) the dimensions chosen for the profile and the scales assigned to them are reasonable and useful in practice; and
(c) to what extent the method may be considered as a systematic procedure for diagnosing the faults in the 'fit' between situation and payment system.

## An Example of the Use of the Procedure

An example is given to illustrate the steps of the procedure and to make explicit the detailed consequences of profile 'misfits'. However, it has to be pointed out that the weaknesses of a firm's payment methods through 'misfit' dimensions do not always take the same form, and this will become apparent later.

Of the various plants investigated I have chosen the Misto Plant to exemplify the use of the method. At the time of this study, management were engaged in examining the scope for increasing the plant's output. The output of the plant had previously been related to an incentive method of payment, though at the time of investigation the operatives were being paid a guaranteed average level of pay. The plant worked a full three shift system and consequently the scope for overtime or further shift working was limited. Though management had an agreed and clearly stated objective in this situation i.e. increase output, their preferences in methods of payment to achieve this objective were subject to much discussion amongst management. The Work Study Department was proposing the reintroduction of a *plant incentive scheme*, though a group of managers thought the area would be better suited to a *measured day work scheme*. Management had already undertaken the first step of the procedure by clearly stating their objective and their preferences in payment — which reflected their values and assumptions and the requirements of this area. The next step was to complete a profile of the area. The Work Study Department undertook the task with the assistance of several other departments within the firm. The operational steps in completing the profile are detailed in the Lupton-Gowler text (and further commented on in the conclusion of this text) and consequently are not elaborated here. The Work Study Department then presented the completed profile of the Misto Plant (Figure 7). We all met to discuss the completed profile and the implications for the two preferred methods of payment. We considered each in turn:

## Incentive Method of Payment?

I began by examining the 'misfit' dimensions on the profile suggesting their possible implications for an incentive scheme. I suggested that the high score on *the degree of automation* (dimension 3) might mean that output is more machine than operator dependent: fluctuations in output and quality would be more dependent on the machine. This would have an effect on bonus payment under an incentive scheme and on the assumptions of such schemes of relating operator effort and reward. *The high rate of product change* (4) (which management said was a frequent cause of job stoppages in this situation) makes the operators highly dependent on changeovers and associated 'indirect' work which in conjunction with the small batch size weakens the effectiveness and directness of the link between operator effort and reward, i.e. these factors are outside their influence but could influence the level of bonus earnings. This circumstance, i.e. high rate of production change, could lead to demands for 'allowances' or the development of 'slack' work values to compensate for variation unrelated to operator effort. The high *incidence of stoppages* (5) at Misto (which are related to product changes) required supervisory assistance for changeovers and adjustments when technical problems developed. If the redeployment of operatives was not possible, or if there were shortcomings in supervisory skill and flexibility, a loss in output might represent a loss of

29

| 1(g) Type of effort | Time | | | Energy | | | Competence | | | |
|---|---|---|---|---|---|---|---|---|---|---|
| 2(g) Unit of accountability | Individual | | | Group | | | Plant | | | |
| | 1 | 2 | 3 | 4 | 5 | 6 | 7 | 8 | 9 | |
| 1 Length of job cycle | to 5 | 6-10 | 11-15 | 16-30 | 31-45 | 46-60 | 61-90 | 91-120 | 121+ | Mins. |
| 2 Number of job modifications | 0 | 1 | 2 | 3 | 4 | 5 | 6 | 7 | 8+ | Av. no. per month |
| 3 Degree of automation | SPT | PAT | SMT | CMT | STM | CTM | SPO | CPO | CCP | |
| 4 Number of product changes | 0 | 1 | 2 | 3 | 4 | 5 | 6 | 7 | 8+ | Av. no. per month |
| 5 Number of job stoppages | 0 | 1 | 2 | 3 | 4 | 5 | 6 | 7 | 8+ | Av. no. per day |
| 6 Duration of job stoppages | 0 | 1-5 | 6-10 | 11-20 | 21-30 | 31-40 | 41-50 | 51-60 | 61+ | Av. no. min per day |
| 7 % job elements specified by management | 71+ | 61-70 | 51-60 | 41-50 | 31-40 | 21-30 | 11-20 | 1-10 | 0 | % |
| 8 % material scrapped | 0 | 1-2 | 3-4 | 5-6 | 7-8 | 9-10 | 11-12 | 13-14 | 15+ | % |
| 9 % products/components rejected | 0 | 1-2 | 3-4 | 5-6 | 7-8 | 9-10 | 11-12 | 13-14 | 15+ | % |
| 10 Time required to fill vacancy | 1 | 2-4 | 5-7 | 8-10 | 11-13 | 14-16 | 17-19 | 20-22 | 23+ | Days |
| 11 Labour stability | 81+ | 71-80 | 61-70 | 51-60 | 41-50 | 31-40 | 21-30 | 11-20 | 0-10 | % |
| 12 Labour turnover | 0 / 0 | 6 / 12 | 12 / 24 | 18 / 36 | 24 / 48 | 30 / 60 | 36 / 72 | 42 / 84 | 48 / 96 | Men % Women % |
| 13 Disputes about pay | 0-4 | 5-8 | 9-12 | 13-16 | 17-20 | 21-24 | 25-28 | 29-32 | 33+ | Av. no. per month |
| 14 Man hours lost in pay disputes | 0-4 | 5-8 | 9-12 | 13-16 | 17-20 | 21-24 | 25-28 | 29-32 | 33+ | % per month |
| 15 % earnings decided outside plant/company | 0-10 | 11-20 | 21-30 | 31-40 | 41-50 | 51-60 | 61-70 | 71-80 | 81+ | % |
| 16 Number of trade unions | 0 | 1-3 | 4-6 | 7-9 | 10-12 | 13-15 | 16-18 | 19-21 | 22+ | All plant |
| 17 Occupational structure | 0-3 | 4-6 | 7-9 | 10-12 | 13-15 | 16-18 | 19-21 | 22-24 | 25+ | All plant |
| 18 Absence | 0 | 2-3 | 4-5 | 6-7 | 8-9 | 10-11 | 12-13 | 14-15 | 16+ | % normal hours |
| 19 Average age of working force | 15-29 | | | 30-44 | | | 45+ | | | Years |
| 20 % labour cost in unit cost | 23+ | 21-23 | 18-20 | 15-17 | 12-14 | 10-12 | 7-9 | 4-6 | 1-3 | % |
| 21 % males in working force | , 0 | to 10 | 11-20 | 21-30 | 31-40 | 41-50 | 51-60 | 61-70 | 71+ | % All plant |

*Figure 7. Profile Of The Misto Plant**

earnings or an additional claim for an allowance. The high *level of material scrapped* (8) is associated with the frequent 'start-up' characteristics of the technology and the small batch sizes produced. The proposed incentive scheme was to include an element of payment related to the percentage of material scrapped. The variability in batch size and improved continuous running of the technology would influence this part of the pay packet in the proposed scheme — which again might be unrelated to operator effort.

It was pointed out by management that dimensions (4), (5), (6) and (8) varied due to slight differences in machine characteristics and batch type. It was suggested that this variation in the machines should be examined to see how representative the profile pattern is — consequently, certain machines might be better suited to an incentive on these particular dimensions than on others. This had not been recognised in the previous incentive scheme.

I also suggested that the *time required to fill a vacancy* (10) would be important if *labour turnover* (12) increased. The time required was said to be primarily due to training requirements rather than labour market constraints. If the training period could be shortened this would improve the effectiveness of the scheme if labour turnover increased.

The high current level of *absence* (18) might weaken the incentive scheme if absence required operatives to be redeployed to machines or products with which they were not familiar. Output might then be lost and disputes about payment might follow. The pay increase associated with the proposed re-introduction of an incentive scheme would (as I saw it) give an even higher level of earnings and possibly further increase the level of absenteeism.

The Misto Plant profile was completed as 'energy' on a 'plant' basis, and the proposed incentive scheme was to apply on a similar basis i.e. a formula based on aggregate allowed and actual hours of output for the total area. But during the discussion of the area and an analysis of product types, management suggested that *accountability* (2g) might have better 'fitted' had it been related to the three main product groups in this area. An improved incentive or incentive schemes would then have been possible by changing the basis

31

of accountability from the 'plant' basis to the main machine — product mixes or by basing it on the work group on each machine.

Another suggestion by management to improve the situational 'fit' was to define the operative's current job. Their argument was that if operative stoppages are due to changeovers and adjustments in setting — up for production runs, which currently required supervisory assistance, these could be made part of the operative's job and consequently improve operator utilisation and free supervision for other work. This would increase the *operative's job cycle,* (1) possibly lower the *percentage of job elements specified by management,* (7) increase the *operator training requirement* (10) and increase supervisory effectiveness (or possibly reduce supervisory costs). However, given the current situation and work relationships the re-introduction of an incentive scheme would foster built-in conflict: as a proposed reduction in the *number and duration of job stoppages* (6) would increase the *rate of product change* (4) and increase the demands on supervision for changeover and development work (i.e. further stoppages). Thus the incentive would increase both the amount of direct (i.e. output paid) work and the 'indirect' work, and any increased output would be constrained by the capacity of the current supervisory system to meet these demands. The substantial 'indirect' work would be a built-in weakness to the operatives' incentive scheme. An analysis of the main reasons for stoppages in the plant gave labour shortages, absence of service and machine or process failure as the most frequent reasons. I asked, how far would the introduction of an incentive method of payment improve these aspects? Three other profile dimensions were 'misfits' on the profile — (15), (17) and (21). The company and union had agreed a pay packet structure and this constrained them in the scope of the alternative structures of the pay packet they could design. The high *occupational structure* (17) score suggests that there is a great deal of scope for 'differential' or 'parity' disputes so that an 'uncontrollable' incentive scheme might substantially multiply labour costs throughout the firm. The last dimension I suggested referred to the fact that *a higher proportion of female labour* (21) would be better suited to an incentive scheme.

We were fortunate at Misto in having the results of a recent survey on operative payment in the plant. This revealed that under the past incentive scheme many of the operatives did not know their own level of output, they were unable to calculate their own 'bonus' earnings and did not think that they in fact could control it, and they recognised that the operatives on some machines had to work harder though this 'effort' was not recognised in payment under the 'plant' incentive scheme. This confirmed the observations made on the difficulty of relating operative reward and effort with their plant level incentive scheme in such a complex situation.

As a further aid to explanation I produced a diagram of the profiled situation to illustrate the context of the pay rules and the impact that this has on the payment system (Figure 8). It is apparent from the dynamic of the system that many of the misfit dimensions influence output *apart* from operative effort and that they are *interdependent*. For example under an incentive scheme a decrease in the rate of product change would reduce stoppages, consequently increase the level of payment which in turn would reduce the current labour turnover.

In the current situation additional payments (e.g. allowances) might well be a necessary part of the pay packet to compensate for circumstances outside the control of the operator. However, if these circumstances were altered through changes in batch size, plant layout, stock levels, supervision and so on the necessity for these additional payments as part of the pay packet might disappear.

### Measured Day Work Method of Payment?

I suggested to the manager at Misto that measured day work might provide a more understandable basis for wages, and improve work measurement and work loading (by a more detailed application of time-study for planning and monitoring effort). This would foster a more critical approach to their management of the current situation i.e. to improve the flow of work rather than building-in such difficulties in the 'allowed time' of the 'work values' that

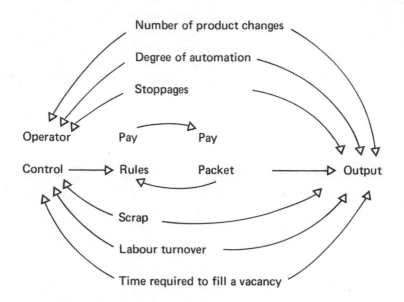

*Figure 8. Diagrammatic Representation Of The Profile Analysis Of The Misto Plant*

then formed the basis of incentive payment. As plant utilisation was currently running at about sixty per cent it might then help clarify the relationship between operator performance and plant utilisation in this situation.

Under this method of payment the reward structure is fixed and management and supervisory skill and administration elicits the 'effort' from the employees. Questions might now be asked about the *output sensitivity*[7] of each of the profile dimensions and the best use of 'operator effort' to increase output. Increased output might come from restructuring certain dimensions of the situation — by

[7] How responsive is output to the movement of each of the profile dimensions and the magnitude of movement on each of the profile dimensions?

improving methods and services and exercising greater control over the sampling and quality control activities that disrupted the current production of the plant. Similarly, fluctuations in output due to the characteristics of the technology, variation in bath sizes, and the incidence of stoppages would now have implications for the management of the 'effort' aspect of the effort-reward relationship *by supervision* and would require a radical change in supervisors' behaviour to sustain the 'effort bargain'.

Under the previous Misto Plant incentive scheme management said that the men had started work late, stopped work early, and had not fully loaded the machines to obtain maximum output. This suggests that the 'energy' scheme had in fact been distorted to become a 'time' scheme. However, as the men were assumed to be working on an incentive scheme there had been little supervisory adjustment to these changes in the situation. It then appeared that the previous plant incentive scheme had failed to relate effort and reward at the individual level. However, the proposed new plant incentive scheme was expected to reduce this lost time and loss of output — primarily by the inclusion of a clause in the written agreement that the men would undertake to fully load the machines. The inclusion of this clause in itself seems to suggest that there was in fact a weak relationship between operative effort and reward and cast doubt on the effectiveness of the new plant incentive. The highest aggregated profile score is non — reciprocal, which in terms of the *original* Lupton-Gowler logic suggests that an incentive payment method is inappropriate. Such a high non-reciprocal profile score favours a consolidated payment method (however, for detailed implication of 'fit' see revised logic in Chapter 4). By working through the implications of the two suggested methods of payment with the profile, a greater appreciation of the costs, constraints and effectiveness of the two schemes in achieving management's objectives was clearly demonstrated in their plant. It is clearly possible to evaluate the values and assumptions about 'operative effort' of those who wished to reintroduce the new plant incentive scheme and those who wished to introduce a measured day work scheme. The possible sequence of change and

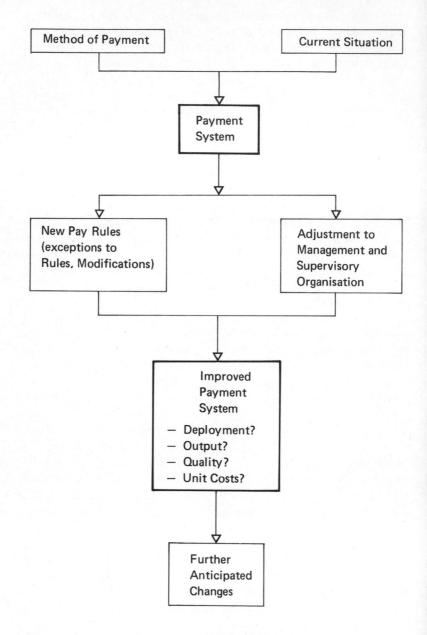

*Figure 9. Possible Sequence Of Change*

36

improvement is illustrated in the following diagram (Figure 9). This, together with the profile, then forms the framework for the final evaluation procedure outlined by Lupton and Gowler.

# 3    The Procedure Applied

The Lupton-Gowler procedure was used in firms in different parts of the country, hence firms were in different labour markets, had different structural characteristics and dispute procedures, and produced a wide range of differing products with differing technologies. The range of products manufactured by the firms was extremely diverse.

In each firm and in each area analysed, information was collected on the firm's objectives of payment, their current method of payment (and recent history on methods of payment), an account of their problems, and the strengths and weaknesses, as seen by management, of the current method of payment. In some cases the profiles were completed by members of the firms and in others they were completed by the author. Most of the firms were seriously considering changing their method of payment. Some were considering consolidating their pay packet structure, e.g. moving from piecework to measured day work, whereas others were differentiating their pay packets, e.g. moving from payment by the hour to incentive bonus schemes.

As the reader may be unfamiliar with the term 'wage drift' used in the text (sometimes also called 'earnings drift'[8] ) this is defined as the total rise in hourly earnings that is unaccounted for in the scheduled (collectively bargained or statutory) hourly rates. This difference in earnings between the national rates of pay and the local plant rate of pay has often been referred to as the 'workplace margin' and is a significant aspect of changes in wage structures and wage movements. 'Drift' often takes two major forms by which

[8] For further discussion of these terms see Tom Lupton *The Management of Earnings and Productivity Drift, Business Management Vol. 97, No. 6, June 1967* and Dan Gowler *Determinants of the Supply of Labour to the Firm, Journal of Management Studies Vol. 6, No. 1. 1969.*

actual earnings move away from expected earnings. Earnings may increase via the growth of the 'variable' element of the pay packet e.g. an increase in the size of the piecework or bonus element of the pay packet — this has sometimes been referred to as 'piecework creep'. Or earnings might increase via 'grade drift', whereby earnings are increased by the process of up-grading — usually this refers to an increase in the size of the 'consolidated' element of the pay packet. Both usually assume (often correctly) that movements in earnings are unrelated to the movement in output, i.e. they describe the type of situation where the payment relationship between effort and reward has deteriorated. However, it is important to be wary of the fact that many of these terms are used by managers in the sense of being 'good' or 'bad' — i.e. the various types of 'drift' may not be necessarily 'bad'. They may be an unintended but useful consequence, or deliberate and controlled way of managing the payment system.

To assist managers to compare their experiences and the uses made of the Lupton-Gowler procedure, a brief introduction is given to the points raised about the payment system and the types of activities and current payment methods diagnosed within each of the following firms. The profile analysis of each is subsequently set out in detail.

## Firm A — Sceptical Ltd.

Could output be increased by introducing an incentive scheme?
An increase in the back-log of work and the union's request for an incentive had led management to consider the introduction of a piecework scheme for its major production areas. Management sought to increase the rate of output, reduce the back-log of work and retain their skilled men.

| | |
|---|---|
| 1. Machine Shop | By the hour |
| 2. Sheet Metal Shop | By the hour |
| 3. Sleeve Shop | By the hour |
| 4. Assembly Shop | By the hour |

## Firm B — Satisfaction Ltd.

An unsatisfactory incentive situation but a satisfactory measured day work situation?
The change of measured day work was considered to be satisfactory by management in terms of their objectives of improving cost forecasting, obtaining an understandable and adaptable wage structure and reducing pay demands for a fixed time period. However, disputes still occurred.

| | |
|---|---|
| 1. High Volume Component Assembly Line | Measured day work |
| 2. Low Volume Complex Equipment Assembly Line | Measured day work |

## Firm C — Non-Financial Rewards Ltd.

Would an incentive improve management's control over their payment system?
Management felt that they were losing control over their payment system, and with a claim for a wage increase they thought that this might be the opportunity to improve their payment system. They were considering whether it might be more appropriate to enlarge jobs, enrich jobs, provide greater job security or staff status rather than just increase payment. However, if they were going to pay out they expected something in return.

| | |
|---|---|
| 1. Component Assembly | Measured day work |
| 2. Machining Flow-line (Heavy items) | Measured day work |
| 3. Machining Flow-line (Small items) | Measured day work |

## Firm D — Management-Union Agreement Ltd.

Payment problems? There are no problems as both top management and senior union officials are in agreement over the methods of payment and wage structure of the firm.

On the particular site examined most of the schemes were incentive (individual and group) schemes; a strong incentive work measurement tradition existed. How appropriate were these past traditions to improving the firm's productivity and how far was the criticism of 'inflexibility' of their payment system reflected in the profile analysis? The local manager's comment forms the basis of this account which seems to differ from the assumptions about operative effort made by those who designed and implemented the firm's incentive schemes.

1. Grinding and Polishing Department     Incentive bonus
2. Melting Department     Incentive bonus
3. Special Hot Press Department     Incentive bonus
4. Diverse Press Department     Incentive bonus

## Firm E — Bargaining Power Ltd.

Escalating earnings, overmanning — union power?

Management currently operated a piece-work method of payment which had given rise to 'wage drift', 'differential disputes' and over-manning. They sought to improve their payment system because it had not only increased their labour costs but also because, as their high earnings levels were used as a reference point on 'parity issues' for their industry, such improvement would assist in the management of the payment systems in other firms. Profile analysis was conducted in three areas of the firm that were subject to rapid 'wage drift'.

1. Assembly Shop     Piecework
2. Paint Shop     Piecework
3. Press Shop     Piecework

41

In application the sequence of steps of the procedure were not adhered to rigidly. Values and assumptions about payment systems tended to be discussed when the situational profile was completed and presented for discussion, particularly when alternative methods of payment were suggested. There seemed to be relatively little evaluation by management of the costs and benefits of holding certain values and assumptions; nor were the stated objectives of a firm necessarily reflected in the payment system design of that firm.

## (A) Sceptical Ltd.

**Could output be increased by introducing an incentive scheme?**

The firm employed one hundred and thirty 'direct' employees who were currently paid by the hour. An increase in the back-log of work and the union's request for an incentive scheme had led management to consider the appropriateness of a piece-work scheme. With this in mind, the following major production units were examined:

1. Machine Shop
2. Assembly Shop
3. Sleeve Shop
4. Sheet Metal Shop

The profiles completed cover the 'direct' workers though all were hourly-paid employees — the distribution and overall profile scores are given on the next page.

The firm's objectives with payment had been and were to
(a) retain their skilled men (consequently their rates of pay were geared to the local rates for skilled men, and pay changes tended to lag this; and
(b) increase the rate of output and reduce the backlog of work.

The firm had a traditional yearly claim for a wage increase, usually based on the firm's rates being behind the district

# The Distribution of Scores

| | Machine Shop | | | Assembly Shop | | | Sleeve Shop | | | Sheet Metal Shop | | |
|---|---|---|---|---|---|---|---|---|---|---|---|---|
| | RI | RD | NR | RI | RD | NR | RI | RD | NR | RI | RD | NR |
| 1 | | | | | | | | | 3 | | | |
| 2 | | 2 | | | 2 | 3 | 3 | | | | 2 | |
| 3 | 3 | | | 3 | | | 1 | | | 3 | | |
| 4 | | | 3 | | | 3 | | | 3 | | | 3 |
| 5 | 2 | | | 2 | | | 3 | | | 2 | | |
| 6 | | 2 | | | 2 | | 3 | | | | 2 | |
| 7 | 2 | | | | 1 | | 3 | | | | | 1 |
| 8 | | 3 | | 2 | | | 3 | | | 2 | | |
| 9 | | 3 | | 2 | | | 3 | | | 2 | | |
| 10 | | | 1 | | | 1 | | | 1 | | | 3 |
| 11 | 3 | | | 3 | | | 3 | | | 3 | | |
| 12 | 2 | | | 3 | | | 1 | | | 3 | | |
| 13 | 3 | | | 3 | | | 3 | | | 3 | | |
| 14 | 3 | | | 3 | | | 3 | | | 3 | | |
| 15 | | | 3 | | | 3 | | | 3 | | | 3 |
| 16 | 2 | | | 2 | | | 2 | | | 2 | | |
| 17 | 3 | | | 3 | | | 3 | | | 3 | | |
| 18 | | 2 | | 1 | | | 2 | | | | | 1 |
| 19 | | | 3 | | 2 | | | 1 | 3 | 3 | | 3 |
| 20 | 3 | | | | 1 | | | | | | | |
| 21 | | | 3 | | | 3 | | | 3 | | | 3 |
| | 26 | 12 | 13(26) | 27 | 8 | 13(26) | 36 | 1 | 16(32) | 29 | 4 | 17(34) |

N.B. The length of the job cycle in the Machine Shop and Sheet Metal Shop is highly variable.

43

## The Overall Profile Scores

|  | Effort | Account-ability | RI | RD | NR |
|---|---|---|---|---|---|
| Machine Shop | Time | Individual | 26 | 12 | 13(26) |
| Sheet Metal Shop | Time | Individual | 29 | 4 | 17(34) |
| Sleeve Shop | Time | Individual | 36 | 1 | 16(32) |
| Assembly Shop | Time | Group | 27 | 8 | 13(26) |

average: however, the union had recently requested an incentive scheme. Management then employed a firm of management consultants to examine the feasibility of an incentive scheme in their current situation and they were advised to introduce a piece-work scheme.

The managers themselves were not satisfied with the 'services' provided to the 'direct' skilled men or the other delays that they were experiencing. They estimated that significant increases in output would come from improving the movement of work to and from the men, i.e. increasing the time the skilled men stayed by their machines without necessarily increasing the skilled man's rate of working. The current large back-log of work was such that progress-chasers were said to be constantly searching for parts and material and not actually progressing work — as did the foremen and many of the operatives who spent their time searching for materials and components as part of the job. The management estimated that between fifteen to twenty per cent of an employee's time was in fact spent preparing the job — 'between-job-time'.

As delivery was an important factor in securing orders the management were anxious about the delays that they experienced for parts and materials from other firms. In order to minimise the impact of these shortages and delays the firm had consequently innovated in design, methods, and substituted materials. Unlike other firms that were similarly restricted (for example, see firm C) they possessed a skilled

44

and flexible labour force to protect themselves against such difficulties — i.e. a capacity to innovate to overcome such constraints.

The works manager had considered how he might measure output in the firm if he were to introduce an output related scheme — and concluded that it would be a difficult problem to measure the output of each man or, in fact, to find any suitable measure. The only method that appeared suitable to him was 'activity rating'. This could be compared with the procedures adopted by other firms for setting 'standards' — time studied work measurement, rate-fixing or the less formalistic procedures by which supervision and management were involved in 'standard' setting. The erosion of payment methods is often attributed to weaknesses of the particular procedure adopted by a firm for establishing standards rather than the situation.

The completed profiles of the four areas of the firm follow and are then commented on (Figures 10, 11, 12 & 13).

In terms of the original Lupton — Gowler logic the profile scores recorded in all of the areas of the firm suggest that it is not a clear-cut case for the application of an incentive scheme; significant non-reciprocal scores are recorded. Certain 'misfit' dimensions exist in *all* areas of the firm, whereas others only exist in certain areas.

The introduction of an incentive scheme into all of the areas analysed might be difficult as the length of the job cycles indicates the high level of skill possessed by the labour force: though at the moment, as the job cycle also includes searching for materials and parts this aspect of the situation would probably have to be 'improved' before an incentive scheme was applied (though this might reduce the length of the job cycle it would still remain long). In particular, the length of the job cycle is long in both the sleeve and assembly shops and is very variable in the machine and sheet metal shops.

In those areas where it is highly variable it might be possible to rationalise this variation into two production units so that the jobs of a short cycle might be grouped together for a better 'fit' with a particular method of payment. In the sheet metal shop the variability in the length

| 1(g) Type of effort | Time | | | Energy | | | Competence | | | |
|---|---|---|---|---|---|---|---|---|---|---|
| 2(g) Unit of accountability | Individual | | | Group | | | Plant | | | |
| | 1 | 2 | 3 | 4 | 5 | 6 | 7 | 8 | 9 | |
| 1 Length of job cycle | to 5 | 6-10 | 11-15 | 16-30 | 31-45 | 46-60 | 61-90 | 91-120 | 121+ | Mins. |
| 2. Number of job modifications | 0 | 1 | 2 | 3 | 4 | 5 | 6 | 7 | 8+ | Av. no. per mon |
| 3 Degree of automation | SPT | PAT | SMT | CMT | STM | CTM | SPO | CPO | CCP | |
| 4 Number of product changes | 0 | 1 | 2 | 3 | 4 | 5 | 6 | 7 | 8+ | Av. no. per mon |
| 5 Number of job stoppages | 0 | 1 | 2 | 3 | 4 | 5 | 6 | 7 | 8+ | Av. no. per day |
| 6 Duration of job stoppages | 0 | 1-5 | 6-10 | 11-20 | 21-30 | 31-40 | 41-50 | 51-60 | 61+ | Av. no. per day |
| 7 % job elements specified by management | 71+ | 61-70 | 51-60 | 41-50 | 31-40 | 21-30 | 11-20 | 1-10 | 0 | % |
| 8 % material scrapped | 0 | 1-2 | 3-4 | 5-6 | 7-8 | 9-10 | 11-12 | 13-14 | 15+ | % |
| 9 % products/components rejected | 0 | 1-2 | 3-4 | 5-6 | 7-8 | 9-10 | 11-12 | 13-14 | 15+ | % |
| 10 Time required to fill vacancy | 1 | 2-4 | 5-7 | 8-10 | 11-13 | 14-16 | 17-19 | 20-22 | 23+ | Days |
| 11 Labour stability | 81+ | 71-80 | 61-70 | 51-60 | 41-50 | 31-40 | 21-30 | 11-20 | 0-10 | % |
| 12 Labour turnover | 0 / 0 | 6 / 12 | 12 / 24 | 18 / 36 | 24 / 48 | 30 / 60 | 36 / 72 | 42 / 84 | 48 / 96 | Men Women |
| 13 Disputes about pay | 0-4 | 5-8 | 9-12 | 13-16 | 17-20 | 21-24 | 25-28 | 29-32 | 33+ | Av. no. per mon |
| 14 Man hours lost in pay disputes | 0-4 | 5-8 | 9-12 | 13-16 | 17-20 | 21-24 | 25-28 | 29-32 | 33+ | % per mon |
| 15 % earnings decided outside plant/company | 0-10 | 11-20 | 21-30 | 31-40 | 41-50 | 51-60 | 61-70 | 71-80 | 81+ | % |
| 16 Number of trade unions | 0 | 1-3 | 4-6 | 7-9 | 10-12 | 13-15 | 16-18 | 19-21 | 22+ | All plant |
| 17 Occupational structure | 0-3 | 4-6 | 7-9 | 10-12 | 13-15 | 16-18 | 19-21 | 22-24 | 25+ | All plant |
| 18 Absence | 0 | 2-3 | 4-5 | 6-7 | 8-9 | 10-11 | 12-13 | 14-15 | 16+ | % normal h |
| 19 Average age of working force | 15-29 | | | 30-44 | | | 45+ | | | Years |
| 20 % labour cost in unit cost | 23+ | 21-23 | 18-20 | 15-17 | 12-14 | 10-12 | 7-9 | 4-6 | 1-3 | % |
| 21 % males in working force | 0 | to 10 | 11-20 | 21-30 | 31-40 | 41-50 | 51-60 | 61-70 | 71+ | % All plant |

*Figure 10. Machine Shop*

46

| | Time | | | Energy | | | Competence | | | |
|---|---|---|---|---|---|---|---|---|---|---|
| **(g) Type of effort** | | | | | | | | | | |
| **(g) Unit of accountability** | Individual | | | Group | | | Plant | | | |
| | **1** | **2** | **3** | **4** | **5** | **6** | **7** | **8** | **9** | |
| Length of job cycle | to 5 | 6-10 | 11-15 | 16-30 | 31-45 | 46-60 | 61-90 | 91-120 | 121+ | Mins. |
| Number of job modifications | 0 | 1 | 2 | 3 | 4 | 5 | 6 | 7 | 8+ | Av. no. per month |
| Degree of automation | SPT | PAT | SMT | CMT | STM | CTM | SPO | CPO | CCP | |
| Number of product changes | 0 | 1 | 2 | 3 | 4 | 5 | 6 | 7 | 8+ | Av. no. per month |
| Number of job stoppages | 0 | 1 | 2 | 3 | 4 | 5 | 6 | 7 | 8+ | Av. no. per day |
| Duration of job stoppages | 0 | 1-5 | 6-10 | 11-20 | 21-30 | 31-40 | 41-50 | 51-60 | 61+ | Av. no. mins. per day |
| % job elements specified by management | 71+ | 61-70 | 51-60 | 41-50 | 31-40 | 21-30 | 11-20 | 1-10 | 0 | % |
| % material scrapped | 0 | 1-2 | 3-4 | 5-6 | 7-8 | 9-10 | 11-12 | 13-14 | 15+ | % |
| % products/components rejected | 0 | 1-2 | 3-4 | 5-6 | 7-8 | 9-10 | 11-12 | 13-14 | 15+ | % |
| Time required to fill vacancy | 1 | 2-4 | 5-7 | 8-10 | 11-13 | 14-16 | 17-19 | 20-22 | 23+ | Days |
| Labour stability | 81+ | 71-80 | 61-70 | 51-60 | 41-50 | 31-40 | 21-30 | 11-20 | 0-10 | % |
| Labour turnover | 0 | 6 | 12 | 18 | 24 | 30 | 36 | 42 | 48 | Men % |
| | 0 | 12 | 24 | 36 | 48 | 60 | 72 | 84 | 96 | Women % |
| Disputes about pay | 0-4 | 5-8 | 9-12 | 13-16 | 17-20 | 21-24 | 25-28 | 29-32 | 33+ | Av. no. per month |
| Man hours lost in pay disputes | 0-4 | 5-8 | 9-12 | 13-16 | 17-20 | 21-24 | 25-28 | 29-32 | 33+ | % per month |
| % earnings decided outside plant/company | 0-10 | 11-20 | 21-30 | 31-40 | 41-50 | 51-60 | 61-70 | 71-80 | 81+ | % |
| Number of trade unions | 0 | 1-3 | 4-6 | 7-9 | 10-12 | 13-15 | 16-18 | 19-21 | 22+ | All plant |
| Occupational structure | 0-3 | 4-6 | 7-9 | 10-12 | 13-15 | 16-18 | 19-21 | 22-24 | 25+ | All plant |
| Absence | 0 | 2-3 | 4-5 | 6-7 | 8-9 | 10-11 | 12-13 | 14-15 | 16+ | % normal hours |
| Average age of working force | 15-29 | | | 30-44 | | | 45+ | | | Years |
| % labour cost in unit cost | 23+ | 21-23 | 18-20 | 15-17 | 12-14 | 10-12 | 7-9 | 4-6 | 1-3 | % |
| % males in working force | 0 | to 10 | 11-20 | 21-30 | 31-40 | 41-50 | 51-60 | 61-70 | 71+ | % All plant |

*Figure 11. Sheet Metal Shop*

47

| | | Time | | | Energy | | | Competence | | | |
|---|---|---|---|---|---|---|---|---|---|---|---|
| 1(g) | Type of effort | | | | | | | | | | |
| 2(g) | Unit of accountability | Individual | | | Group | | | Plant | | | |
| | | 1 | 2 | 3 | 4 | 5 | 6 | 7 | 8 | 9 | |
| 1 | Length of job cycle | to 5 | 6-10 | 11-15 | 16-30 | 31-45 | 46-60 | 61-90 | 91-120 | 121+ | Mins. |
| 2 | Number of job modifications | 0 | 1 | 2 | 3 | 4 | 5 | 6 | 7 | 8+ | Av. no. per month |
| 3 | Degree of automation | SPT | PAT | SMT | CMT | STM | CTM | SPO | CPO | CCP | |
| 4 | Number of product changes | 0 | 1 | 2 | 3 | 4 | 5 | 6 | 7 | 8+ | Av. no. per month |
| 5 | Number of job stoppages | 0 | 1 | 2 | 3 | 4 | 5 | 6 | 7 | 8+ | Av. no. per day |
| 6 | Duration of job stoppages | 0 | 1-5 | 6-10 | 11-20 | 21-30 | 31-40 | 41-50 | 51-60 | 61+ | Av. no. mins per day |
| 7 | % job elements specified by management | 71+ | 61-70 | 51-60 | 41-50 | 31-40 | 21-30 | 11-20 | 1-10 | 0 | % |
| 8 | % material scrapped | 0 | 1-2 | 3-4 | 5-6 | 7-8 | 9-10 | 11-12 | 13-14 | 15+ | % |
| 9 | % products/components rejected | 0 | 1-2 | 3-4 | 5-6 | 7-8 | 9-10 | 11-12 | 13-14 | 15+ | % |
| 10 | Time required to fill vacancy | 1 | 2-4 | 5-7 | 8-10 | 11-13 | 14-16 | 17-19 | 20-22 | 23+ | Days |
| 11 | Labour stability | 81+ | 71-80 | 61-70 | 51-60 | 41-50 | 31-40 | 21-30 | 11-20 | 0-10 | % |
| 12 | Labour turnover | 0 | 6 | 12 | 18 | 24 | 30 | 36 | 42 | 48 | Men % |
| | | 0 | 12 | 24 | 36 | 48 | 60 | 72 | 84 | 96 | Women % |
| 13 | Disputes about pay | 0-4 | 5-8 | 9-12 | 13-16 | 17-20 | 21-24 | 25-28 | 29-32 | 33+ | Av. no. per month |
| 14 | Man hours lost in pay disputes | 0-4 | 5-8 | 9-12 | 13-16 | 17-20 | 21-24 | 25-28 | 29-32 | 33+ | % per month |
| 15 | % earnings decided outside plant/company | 0-10 | 11-20 | 21-30 | 31-40 | 41-50 | 51-60 | 61-70 | 71-80 | 81+ | % |
| 16 | Number of trade unions | 0 | 1-3 | 4-6 | 7-9 | 10-12 | 13-15 | 16-18 | 19-21 | 22+ | All plant |
| 17 | Occupational structure | 0-3 | 4-6 | 7-9 | 10-12 | 13-15 | 16-18 | 19-21 | 22-24 | 25+ | All plant |
| 18 | Absence | 0 | 2-3 | 4-5 | 6-7 | 8-9 | 10-11 | 12-13 | 14-15 | 16+ | % normal hour |
| 19 | Average age of working force | 15-29 | | | 30-44 | | | 45+ | | | Years |
| 20 | % labour cost in unit cost | 23+ | 21-23 | 18-20 | 15-17 | 12-14 | 10-12 | 7-9 | 4-6 | 1-3 | % |
| 21 | % males in working force | 0 | to 10 | 11-20 | 21-30 | 31-40 | 41-50 | 51-60 | 61-70 | 71+ | % All plant |

*Figure 12. Sleeve Shop*

48

| | Time | | | Energy | | | Competence | | | |
|---|---|---|---|---|---|---|---|---|---|---|
| g) Type of effort | | | | | | | | | | |
| g) Unit of accountability | Individual | | | Group | | | Plant | | | |
| | 1 | 2 | 3 | 4 | 5 | 6 | 7 | 8 | 9 | |
| Length of job cycle | to 5 | 6-10 | 11-15 | 16-30 | 31-45 | 46-60 | 61-90 | 91-120 | 121+ | Mins. |
| Number of job modifications | 0 | 1 | 2 | 3 | 4 | 5 | 6 | 7 | 8+ | Av. no. per month |
| Degree of automation | SPT | PAT | SMT | CMT | STM | CTM | SPO | CPO | CCP | |
| Number of product changes | 0 | 1 | 2 | 3 | 4 | 5 | 6 | 7 | 8+ | Av. no. per month |
| Number of job stoppages | 0 | 1 | 2 | 3 | 4 | 5 | 6 | 7 | 8+ | Av. no. per day |
| Duration of job stoppages | 0 | 1-5 | 6-10 | 11-20 | 21-30 | 31-40 | 41-50 | 51-60 | 61+ | Av. no. mins per day |
| % job elements specified by management | 71+ | 61-70 | 51-60 | 41-50 | 31-40 | 21-30 | 11-20 | 1-10 | 0 | % |
| % material scrapped | 0 | 1-2 | 3-4 | 5-6 | 7-8 | 9-10 | 11-12 | 13-14 | 15+ | % |
| % products/components rejected | 0 | 1-2 | 3-4 | 5-6 | 7-8 | 9-10 | 11-12 | 13-14 | 15+ | % |
| Time required to fill vacancy | 1 | 2-4 | 5-7 | 8-10 | 11-13 | 14-16 | 17-19 | 20-22 | 23+ | Days |
| Labour stability | 81+ | 71-80 | 61-70 | 51-60 | 41-50 | 31-40 | 21-30 | 11-20 | 0-10 | % |
| Labour turnover | 0 | 6 | 12 | 18 | 24 | 30 | 36 | 42 | 48 | Men % |
| | 0 | 12 | 24 | 36 | 48 | 60 | 72 | 84 | 96 | Women % |
| Disputes about pay | 0-4 | 5-8 | 9-12 | 13-16 | 17-20 | 21-24 | 25-28 | 29-32 | 33+ | Av. no. per month |
| Man hours lost in pay disputes | 0-4 | 5-8 | 9-12 | 13-16 | 17-20 | 21-24 | 25-28 | 29-32 | 33+ | % per month |
| % earnings decided outside plant/company | 0-10 | 11-20 | 21-30 | 31-40 | 41-50 | 51-60 | 61-70 | 71-80 | 81+ | % |
| Number of trade unions | 0 | 1-3 | 4-6 | 7-9 | 10-12 | 13-15 | 16-18 | 19-21 | 22+ | All plant |
| Occupational structure | 0-3 | 4-6 | 7-9 | 10-12 | 13-15 | 16-18 | 19-21 | 22-24 | 25+ | All plant |
| Absence | 0 | 2-3 | 4-5 | 6-7 | 8-9 | 10-11 | 12-13 | 14-15 | 16+ | % normal hours |
| Average age of working force | 15-29 | | | 30-44 | | | 45+ | | | Years |
| % labour cost in unit cost | 23+ | 21-23 | 18-20 | 15-17 | 12-14 | 10-12 | 7-9 | 4-6 | 1-3 | % |
| % males in working force | 0 | to 10 | 11-20 | 21-30 | 31-40 | 41-50 | 51-60 | 61-70 | 71+ | % All plant |

*Figure 13. Assembly Shop*

49

of the job cycle is related to the number of product changes and job modifications, and so here one might examine the factors that influence these two dimensions and their relation to the incidence of job stoppages, in order to reduce this instability in the situation.

An incentive scheme would also have to deal with the 'misfit' dimension of the high rate of product change which reflects the jobbing nature of production in this firm and the constant improvement, modification and development of product design in the production areas. As an increase in the pace of work would also increase the rate of product change there would then be a degree of built-in conflict with an incentive scheme that sought to save time i.e. reduce dimensions (4) and (5).

Improved situational 'fit' might be possible if product design and development activities were separated from the production areas, increasing use was made of standardised parts in product design, and higher levels of stock held. In the machine shop the high rate of product change is related to the high scrap and reject levels — a lower rate of product change would also improve the 'incentive' fit on these two dimensions. Though stockholding was possible in some areas, management said that it was prohibitive in the sleeve shop as raw material costs represented a very high proportion of total unit cost. This then suggests that a material utilisation incentive might be appropriate, though the sleeve shop profile indicates that scrapped material is insignificant in this area.

An incentive scheme in the situation of this firm would also require greater specification of the job by management or supervision. This would probably prove very difficult and costly with the current low specification, long job cycles and high rates of product change in *all* of the areas. It was not surprising that the works manager thought it would be difficult to measure output in this situation. The cost of establishing and maintaining 'standards' by any method would be extremely difficult. On the whole the situation might have been a better fit on several of the technological dimensions had improvements in production scheduling, and technical and design services been effected.

50

The profile score on the labour turnover dimension indicates that the labour market was having an impact in the machine shop and sleeve shop at the time, the effect being compounded by the long time required to fill a vacancy. A reduction of labour turnover in the sleeve and machine shops would improve the firm's output. In the past, adjustments to labour market pressures had been met by the adjustment of time-rates (in accordance with the yearly claim) and by the provision of overtime. The introduction of an incentive scheme might have combated the current labour market pressure by providing higher earnings — an adjustment to the time — rates or overtime would have had the same effect on the labour turnover dimension. The firm's usual policy was to recruit skilled men who were now becoming difficult to retain. To improve this situational 'fit' management had considered the recruitment of more apprentices so as to reduce their labour market vulnerability and adjust the firm's ageing labour force which also contributed to their pattern of absence in some areas.

In terms of percentage of labour costs in total unit costs, the potential benefits of improved payment 'fit' would be greater in the machine and sheet metal shops than in the other shops — though at the moment, in terms of the Lupton-Gowler logic, the profiles indicate that the sleeve shop is the closest 'fit' to an incentive situation.

### Conclusion for Sceptical Ltd.

Given the current profile patterns, an incentive scheme in this situation would probably require substantial administration and the question might arise about the 'economics' of fixing a rate for the job. The incentive pay packet structure that would develop in such a situation would be one characterised by a large percentage of hours on 'covered time' or 'average payment', or the development of generous piece-rates to compensate for variations in the work situation not accounted for by the 'performance standards'.

In terms of the firm's stated objectives of retaining their skilled labour and increasing output, an incentive scheme is not the simple answer to retention and improved productivity in their particular situation. The firm might be compared with most of the others for its time-rates (and the overtime opportunities provided) gave management a degree of flexibility in using its labour force which others were paying for by substantial administrative overheads in running incentive schemes, additional 'premiums' and 'allowances' and 'grade drift' — if not constant disputes about pay that arose when the circumstances of the job situation changed (see firms C and D in particular). Payment by the hour in this situation gave supervision and management a great deal of flexibility in a dynamic situation which required them to innovate to overcome shortages and delays in meeting delivery dates.

It is not known on what basis the external consultants had evaluated the appropriateness of a piece-work scheme. The use of the profile method of evaluation illustrated the possible consequences of having the 'misfit' dimensions with an incentive scheme and the firm's management were sufficiently satisfied to reject the consultants' 'package' recommendations of an incentive scheme, and attempt to improve output in their situation through improved supervisory and managerial efforts rather than rely on the introduction of a piecework scheme to meet their objectives.

## (B) Satisfaction Ltd.

**An unsatisfactory incentive situation but a satisfactory measured day work situation?**

This firm employed a total of three thousand manual employees. Like firm C they had experienced rapid growth in the size of their labour force. They currently operated from four sites which were only a few miles apart and were said to operate as autonomous divisions though, of course, they were subject to the same labour market constraints. Management said that the payment system had been unsatisfactory when they possessed a number of incentive schemes for their 'direct' workers; however, having changed to measured day work they were now generally satisfied with their payment method.

The previous payment schemes were a mixture of three types:

1. Basic rate and 'incentive' bonus — for the assembly shop
2. Basic rate and 'lieu' bonus — for the machine shop
3. Basic plus 'merit' awards — for other shops

The assembly shop was originally manned by a predominantly female labour force paid on an incentive bonus scheme. This scheme was said to have kept 'running away' i.e. earnings increased but output did not. This was not only dysfunctional in escalating unit labour costs in the assembly shop, but as the firm was later to expand, primarily by recruiting more men into the machine shop, the 'skilled man's differential' was constantly being eroded and this erosion was becoming increasingly costly to readjust. Under this pressure, work study introduced a 'lieu bonus' scheme to maintain the skilled and semi-skilled differential. However, earnings still increased in the assembly shop and so in order to maintain differentials with *other* production areas in the firm and to retain some of their skilled labour, they also introduced a 'merit-rating' scheme to manage the payment system. However, the firm's system of payment rapidly became meaningless as 'wage drift' further increased via the 'loose bonus' and increased merit awards resulting from successful operative pressure tactics on the foremen who adminstered the merit rating scheme. In order to cope with the constant demands for money and consequent differential leap-frogging between the various groups, the firm then changed to measured day work and long-term fixed agreements with their trade unions. The firm's work study officer said that he considered the major reason for the failure of the firm's incentive bonus schemes in the assembly areas was due to the problem of setting 'values' where there were large fluctuations in batch sizes produced — in profile terms the situation would score high on the rate of product change (dimension 4). Now management considered that they were able to measure much better than previously — which was usually in response to complaints about payment – and had improved work loading and increased the coverage of time-study measurement. They were satisfied with the new scheme.

The objectives the firm had sought with their payment system and which they considered they had achieved with their scheme were to

(a) achieve a satisfactory basis for forecasting costs.
(b) obtain an understandable and adaptable wage structure
(c) reduce union pay demands to negotiating once for fixed time period.

It was decided to conduct the profile analysis in two areas of the assembly shop in order to examine the characteristics of a previously unsatisfactory incentive bonus situation and a currently satisfactory measured day work situation. The two areas analysed by the Lupton-Gowler method and the profile scores were as follows:

| | Effort | Account-ability | RI | RD | NR |
|---|---|---|---|---|---|
| (1) High Volume Component Assembly Line | Energy | Individual | 25 | 4 | 44 |
| (2) Low Volume Complex Equipment Assembly Line | Energy | Individual | 20 | 2 | 56 |

Both score *very highly* on non-reciprocal scores which in terms of the original Lupton-Gowler logic suggests that a 'consolidated' rather than 'incentive' pay packet is appropriate.

| 1(g) Type of effort | Time | | | Energy | | | Competence | | | |
|---|---|---|---|---|---|---|---|---|---|---|
| 2(g) Unit of accountability | Individual | | | Group | | | Plant | | | |
| | 1 | 2 | 3 | 4 | 5 | 6 | 7 | 8 | 9 | |
| 1 Length of job cycle | to 5 | 6-10 | 11-15 | 16-30 | 31-45 | 46-60 | 61-90 | 91-120 | 121+ | Mins. |
| 2 Number of job modifications | 0 | 1 | 2 | 3 | 4 | 5 | 6 | 7 | 8+ | Av. no. per month |
| 3 Degree of automation | SPT | PAT | SMT | CMT | STM | CTM | SPO | CPO | CCP | |
| 4 Number of product changes | 0 | 1 | 2 | 3 | 4 | 5 | 6 | 7 | 8+ | Av. no. per month |
| 5 Number of job stoppages | 0 | 1 | 2 | 3 | 4 | 5 | 6 | 7 | 8+ | Av. no. per day |
| 6 Duration of job stoppages | 0 | 1-5 | 6-10 | 11-20 | 21-30 | 31-40 | 41-50 | 51-60 | 61+ | Av. no. mins. per day |
| 7 % job elements specified by management | 71+ | 61-70 | 51-60 | 41-50 | 31-40 | 21-30 | 11-20 | 1-10 | 0 | % |
| 8 % material scrapped | 0 | 1-2 | 3-4 | 5-6 | 7-8 | 9-10 | 11-12 | 13-14 | 15+ | % |
| 9 % products/components rejected | 0 | 1-2 | 3-4 | 5-6 | 7-8 | 9-10 | 11-12 | 13-14 | 15+ | % |
| 10 Time required to fill vacancy | 1 | 2-4 | 5-7 | 8-10 | 11-13 | 14-16 | 17-19 | 20-22 | 23+ | Days |
| 11 Labour stability | 81+ | 71-80 | 61-70 | 51-60 | 41-50 | 31-40 | 21-30 | 11-20 | 0-10 | % |
| 12 Labour turnover | 0 / 0 | 6 / 12 | 12 / 24 | 18 / 36 | 24 / 48 | 30 / 60 | 36 / 72 | 42 / 84 | 48 / 96 | Men % Women % |
| 13 Disputes about pay | 0-4 | 5-8 | 9-12 | 13-16 | 17-20 | 21-24 | 25-28 | 29-32 | 33+ | Av. no. per month |
| 14 Man hours lost in pay disputes | 0-4 | 5-8 | 9-12 | 13-16 | 17-20 | 21-24 | 25-28 | 29-32 | 33+ | % per month |
| 15 % earnings decided outside plant/company | 0-10 | 11-20 | 21-30 | 31-40 | 41-50 | 51-60 | 61-70 | 71-80 | 81+ | %- |
| 16 Number of trade unions | 0 | 1-3 | 4-6 | 7-9 | 10-12 | 13-15 | 16-18 | 19-21 | 22+ | All plant |
| 17 Occupational structure | 0-3 | 4-6 | 7-9 | 10-12 | 13-15 | 16-18 | 19-21 | 22-24 | 25+ | All plant |
| 18 Absence | 0 | 2-3 | 4-5 | 6-7 | 8-9 | 10-11 | 12-13 | 14-15 | 16+ | % normal hours |
| 19 Average age of working force | 15-29 | | | 30-44 | | | 45+ | | | Years |
| 20 % labour cost in unit cost | 23+ | 21-23 | 18-20 | 15-17 | 12-14 | 10-12 | 7-9 | 4-6 | 1-3 | % |
| 21 % males in working force | 0 | to 10 | 11-20 | 21-30 | 31-40 | 41-50 | 51-60 | 61-70 | 71+ | % All plant |

*As management-union agreement applied to all four sites these particular dimensions were scored on that basis.

*Figure 14. High Volume Small Component Assembly Line*

### High Volume Compenent Assembly Line.

In this area management paid particular attention to operator performance as labour costs were more important than the costs of stock-holding, scrap and so on. The labour force was stable and rarely redeployed outside its particular work area, consequently the area was more self-contained than that of the complex equipment assembly line. The component assembly line's stability was in part also attributed to the high level of operator skill, and supervisory skill and flexibility as well as the additional buffers of high stock levels. Supervision was able to change the type of products produced, introduce modifications and cope with volume fluctuations with apparently little disruption to production (see firms C and D). The high rate of product change, modifications and fluctuations in volume were managed by well-informed, skilled and highly rewarded supervision who were kept informed of their future work load and their costs and were constantly involved in objective setting exercises and reviews of their progress in meeting targets and standards. 'Misfit' profile dimensions (2), (4), (5), (9) and (18) which might have disrupted an incentive scheme and restructured the incentive pay packet, were effectively monitored and adjusted to with no loss of earnings to the operator, and in this situation with perhaps little loss of 'effort' (output) from the substained supervisory and management organisation. Under an incentive scheme such 'misfit' dimensions might have given rise to erratic earnings, restriction of output and frequent disputes about pay. The 'effort' aspect under this method of payment was maintained by supervisors' rulings and procedures rather than the fixed and often centralised rules of relating 'effort' and 'reward' with the payment schemes of some firms.

### Low Volume Complex Equipment Assembly Line.

Assembly work in this situation was subject to more significant fluctuations in inventory and manning than the small component assembly line, and though supervision and management of the area was itself very skilled and flexible, it could not meet the priorities of this area with the resources contained within the line. The level of work in progress was a

56

| Type of effort | Time | | | Energy | | | Competence | | | |
|---|---|---|---|---|---|---|---|---|---|---|
| Unit of accountability | Individual | | | Group | | | Plant | | | |
| | 1 | 2 | 3 | 4 | 5 | 6 | 7 | 8 | 9 | |
| Length of job cycle | to 5 | 6-10 | 11-15 | 16-30 | 31-45 | 46-60 | 61-90 | 91-120 | 121+ | Mins. |
| Number of job modifications | 0 | 1 | 2 | 3 | 4 | 5 | 6 | 7 | 8+ | Av. no. per month |
| Degree of automation | SPT | PAT | SMT | CMT | STM | CTM | SPO | CPO | CCP | |
| Number of product changes | 0 | 1 | 2 | 3 | 4 | 5 | 6 | 7 | 8+ | Av. no. per month |
| Number of job stoppages | 0 | 1 | 2 | 3 | 4 | 5 | 6 | 7 | 8+ | Av. no. per day |
| Duration of job stoppages | 0 | 1-5 | 6-10 | 11-20 | 21-30 | 31-40 | 41-50 | 51-60 | 61+ | Av. no. mins. per day |
| % job elements specified by management | 71+ | 61-70 | 51-60 | 41-50 | 31-40 | 21-30 | 11-20 | 1-10 | 0 | % |
| % material scrapped | 0 | 1-2 | 3-4 | 5-6 | 7-8 | 9-10 | 11-12 | 13-14 | 15+ | % |
| % products/components rejected | 0 | 1-2 | 3-4 | 5-6 | 7-8 | 9-10 | 11-12 | 13-14 | 15+ | % |
| Time required to fill vacancy | 1 | 2-4 | 5-7 | 8-10 | 11-13 | 14-16 | 17-19 | 20-22 | 23+ | Days |
| Labour stability | 81+ | 71-80 | 61-70 | 51-60 | 41-50 | 31-40 | 21-30 | 11-20 | 0-10 | % |
| Labour turnover | 0 | 6 | 12 | 18 | 24 | 30 | 36 | 42 | 48 | Men % |
| | 0 | 12 | 24 | 36 | 48 | 60 | 72 | 84 | 96 | Women % |
| Disputes about pay | 0-4 | 5-8 | 9-12 | 13-16 | 17-20 | 21-24 | 25-28 | 29-32 | 33+ | Av. no. per month |
| Man hours lost in pay disputes | 0-4 | 5-8 | 9-12 | 13-16 | 17-20 | 21-24 | 25-28 | 29-32 | 33+ | % per month |
| % earnings decided outside plant/company | 0-10 | 11-20 | 21-30 | 31-40 | 41-50 | 51-60 | 61-70 | 71-80 | 81+ | % |
| Number of trade unions | 0 | 1-3 | 4-6 | 7-9 | 10-12 | 13-15 | 16-18 | 19-21 | 22+ | All plant |
| Occupational structure | 0-3 | 4-6 | 7-9 | 10-12 | 13-15 | 16-18 | 19-21 | 22-24 | 25+ | All plant |
| Absence | 0 | 2-3 | 4-5 | 6-7 | 8-9 | 10-11 | 12-13 | 14-15 | 16+ | % normal hours |
| Average age of working force | 15-29 | | | 30-44 | | | 45+ | | | Years |
| % labour cost in unit cost | 23+ | 21-23 | 18-20 | 15-17 | 12-14 | 10-12 | 7-9 | 4-6 | 1-3 | % |
| % males in working force | 0 | to 10 | 11-20 | 21-30 | 31-40 | 41-50 | 51-60 | 61-70 | 71+ | % All plant |

*Figure 15. Low Volume Equipment Assembly Line*

57

greater cost than the associated labour costs in assembly and consequently the emphasis was less on operator performance and more on 'building what you have parts for'. Supply constraints meant that inventory levels fluctuated a great deal and to meet these periodic crises, operatives were deployed into the area. In the previous area the customer was sensitive to the cost of the components, but in this area delivery was considered to be most important and delivery dates had to be met even at the cost of disrupted production and the subsequent under-utilisation of resources (e.g. labour) in meeting deadlines (compare this with the objectives and situations of firms C and A). The low volume, higher degree of customer specification of the final design of the equipment, the stock and supply difficulties, and the firm's delivery commitments contributed to the resultant profile pattern of this situation. The supervisory and managerial emphasis in this situation was to improve the flow of work by redeployment, method innovation, layout design, analysing down-time, together with objective-setting exercises on their current problems. Here, management carried the cost of under-utilising labour to meet its objectives with the fixed reward structure, whereas in other firms men's incentive earnings were often penalised and brought operatives into conflict with management's object-ives and requirements for flexibility.

### Conclusion For Satisfaction Ltd.

In this firm management recognised that in some situations operatives' efforts should not be penalised if management created or was itself restricted by circumstances that they could not control — requiring for example substantial redeployment, high rates of product change or high reject levels (compare this with firm D). Their payment method allowed them to cope with rapid product change, vary batch sizes and deal with restrictions in the workflow with little interference from their consolidated payment method. It is apparent that their monitoring of operative 'effort' includes aspects that in other firms would be built-in to their 'work values' or not even be recognised or allowed for in the payment rules of some firms. The supervisory role and associated productivity and advisory service in this firm was highly developed. Supervisors were usually recruited from the work study section of the firm and had access to the cost and performance data of their area. They were involved in continuous objective-setting exercise in conjunction with management and a central productivity service. Unlike some of the other firms, management and supervision were well aware of the impact of many of the profile dimensions on output (effort).

The high non-reciprocal scores on both the profiles suggest a consolidated level of payment (reward) and in this firm it is associated with an 'energy' type of scheme — which on occasions with development work, or in a restricted situation, is probably in fact 'time' — though management could, in fact, establish and re-establish performance requirements when and where required to match their objectives. Profile dimension (4), the rate of product change did appear to be important in one area but it was not the only 'misfit' dimension that might have given rise to the 'loosening' of the previous incentive bonus scheme. The level of job modifications, stoppages, re-work, labour stability (with long training requirements) and levels of absence all contributed to weakening the 'effort bargain' under fixed incentive rules. With the current payment method the link between 'effort' and 'reward' was maintained by flexible supervisory rulings in the situation.

Their method of payment and type of agreement (a fixed-period agreement) had given them a relatively stable wage structure compared with the movements in the wage structures of other firms (primarily on incentive schemes) in their locality. Their labour costs were then known and constant for a fixed period, and with their particular grade structure there was no possibility of 'grade drift' (see firm C). As their pay rates were relatively better for most of the types of skilled and unskilled labour they employed in their labour market, this rigidity in their pay structure might be considered to be well suited to their objectives and the maintenance of the 'effort bargain' with this method of payment. However, if the labour market had radically and rapidly changed they might have faced substantial difficulties — increased overtime payment and a loss of 'effort' might have been the only short-term adjustments possible. Similarly, if they had been required to innovate technically, requiring skills in short supply, management might have found their fixed and agreed grade structure a major constraint, whereas, for example in firm C, the 'grade drift' of their grade structure (facilitated by a 'skill and flexibility' points systems) and 'wage drift' (facilitated by 'additional' payments) provided some 'automatic adjustment' in dealing with their labour market difficulties and their restricted production situation.

Although firm B's management had expressed general satisfaction with their method payment, disputes still occurred — usually related to the 'effort' part of the effort-reward relation with this method of payment. For example, disputes occurred over:

1. Those changes of the job cycle (e.g. from technical change) that increased the pace of the work. The degree of automation was still a 'misfit' dimension.

2. The greater flexibility which allowed a greater range of comparison of work 'effort', and claims were made that they should be paid more than others, or should be paid as much as others (i.e. 'parity' or 'differentials' in 'effort'.) The complexity of the occupational structure continued to provide a strong bargaining point.

3. New labour introduced into those parts of the firm where work was being 'developed' claimed bonus rewards for 'bonus' efforts as 'development' was completed. They were informed that they were already being paid for 'bonus' efforts. The redeployment of labour into 'developing' production situations still proved to be difficult situations in which to maintain the effort-reward relation with their payment method.

60

Disputes still occurred over the 'misfit' nature of the situation, though they were less then they had experienced with their previous incentive scheme. The relation between reward and effort seemed to be better managed by supervision and management rather than by incentive payment rules (and the constant situational requirement to repeatedly change or adjust such rules). Consolidated payment also meant that operative earnings (level and stability) were not penalised when management objectives differed or changed in the different areas of the firm.

Management's satisfaction with its current payment system probably reflects the marked reduction in disputes about pay (dimensions 13 and 14) and their related effect on the other dimensions of the situation, and the improvement in managerial skills and procedures to reduce or manage the still significant number of misfit dimensions rather. than to presume operative effort alone was sufficient to deal with the firm's circumstances.

## (C) Non-Financial Rewards Ltd.

**Would an incentive improve management's control over the payment system?**

This was a relatively new factory. Management had increased both the production facilities and the labour force rapidly and they planned further expansion. The plant had been designed for, and primarily manned by, an unskilled labour force, and was organised on a one union, one plant basis. Management had used measured day work as their method of payment for six hundred 'direct' workers since the factory had started production. The factory was originally designed to produce large volumes of two new products which market research assessments had predicted would be in demand. However, it was soon apparent (after the factory had been set up) that the original market research projections were inaccurate. The firm was then forced into changing its product policy. It began to manufacture a larger range of products suitable for a diverse range of applications instead of the original two standard products.

A review of payment was prompted by a recent approach by the trade union for a wage increase and by management's increasing dissatisfaction with the current method of payment. These two circumstances seemed to offer an opportunity to improve or change their method of payment. Other changes were also considered e.g. whether it might be more appropriate to enlarge jobs, enrich jobs, provide greater job security or staff status rather than just increasing payment; however, if management were going to pay out they expected something in return.

Dissatisfaction with their current method of payment arose from management's assessment that they were losing control over their payment system as:

(a) line production management and supervision were reluctant to take issue over the low levels of output.
(b) reporting by foremen was considered to be a weakness in the control mechanism.
(c) labour turnover was increasing.
(d) the current differential between the skilled and unskilled in the union was considered likely to precipitate a dispute about the appropriateness of the grade structure.

The unskilled were the most numerically powerful in the union but in this case least valued in the labour market. There were pressures *within* the skilled and unskilled categories to attempt to negotiate separately. This threatened management's current method of payment as it was related to an agreed job grade structure. The 'weakness' in foremen reporting apparently made it possible to book 'lost time' in such a way as to keep operator efficiency looking good, i.e. most foremen were judged on this method of control which it was claimed was easy to 'fiddle', whereas, in other parts of the factory, other foremen would indicate the work completed rather than produce these 'nice reports'.

The agreed job evaluation grade structure in firm C was based on a 'points' system. Operatives under this system were paid various consolidated rates though they could obtain additional payment for skill and flexibility and overtime. The industrial relations adviser said that the shop stewards currently used the firm's job evaluation scheme as a basis for negotiating wages, and if men were near the top of their grade they would try to discover changes in their job specification or listen for new instructions from the foremen so as to gain more points and so move up the structure. Unlike the job evaluation scheme in firm B, it was then possible in this firm to move up the grade structure if any significant changes occurred in a man's job, though the grade structure itself was only negotiated once a year. There was then little problem in transferring or changing a man's work since this flexibility gave him additional points. Consequently should changes in the situation require re-deployment, for example, with labour shortages or material shortages, earnings 'automatically' increased.

It was decided to assess the following typical areas of the firm by profile analysis:


1. Machining Flow-line (small part items)
2. Machining Flow-line (heavy items)
3. Component Assembly

and the profile scores obtained in these areas were as follows:

|     | Effort | Accountability | RI | RD | NR |
| --- | ------ | -------------- | -- | -- | -- |
| (1) | Energy | Group | 29 | 9 | 26 |
| (2) | Energy | Group | 25 | 12 | 30 |
| (3) | Energy | Group | 22 | 17 | 37 |

During discussions managers said that as there was a strong preference amongst the 'direct' production workers for a day scheme that related reward and effort, they had therefore considered the possibility of introducing an incentive to solve their current problems. But in many of the production areas of the firm, they themselves recognised that the high product

| 1(g) | Type of effort | Time | | | Energy | | | Competence | | | |
|---|---|---|---|---|---|---|---|---|---|---|---|
| 2(g) | Unit of accountability | Individual | | | Group | | | Plant | | | |
| | | 1 | 2 | 3 | 4 | 5 | 6 | 7 | 8 | 9 | |
| 1 | Length of job cycle | to 5 | 6-10 | 11-15 | 16-30 | 31-45 | 46-60 | 61-90 | 91-120 | 121+ | Mins. |
| 2. | Number of job modifications | 0 | 1 | 2 | 3 | 4 | 5 | 6 | 7 | 8+ | Av. no. per mon |
| 3 | Degree of automation | SPT | PAT | SMT | CMT | STM | CTM | SPO | CPO | CCP | |
| 4 | Number of product changes | 0 | 1 | 2 | 3 | 4 | 5 | 6 | 7 | 8+ | Av. no. per mon |
| 5 | Number of job stoppages | 0 | 1 | 2 | 3 | 4 | 5 | 6 | 7 | 8+ | Av. no. per day |
| 6 | Duration of job stoppages | 0 | 1-5 | 6-10 | 11-20 | 21-30 | 31-40 | 41-50 | 51-60 | 61+ | Av. no. per day |
| 7 | % job elements specified by management | 71+ | 61-70 | 51-60 | 41-50 | 31-40 | 21-30 | 11-20 | 1-10 | 0 | % |
| 8 | % material scrapped | 0 | 1-2 | 3-4 | 5-6 | 7-8 | 9-10 | 11-12 | 13-14 | 15+ | % |
| 9 | % products/components rejected | 0 | 1-2 | 3-4 | 5-6 | 7-8 | 9-10 | 11-12 | 13-14 | 15+ | % |
| 10 | Time required to fill vacancy | 1 | 2-4 | 5-7 | 8-10 | 11-13 | 14-16 | 17-19 | 20-22 | 23+ | Days |
| 11 | Labour stability | 81+ | 71-80 | 61-70 | 51-60 | 41-50 | 31-40 | 21-30 | 11-20 | 0-10 | % |
| 12 | Labour turnover | 0 | 6 | 12 | 18 | 24 | 30 | 36 | 42 | 48 | Men |
| | | 0 | 12 | 24 | 36 | 48 | 60 | 72 | 84 | 96 | Women |
| 13 | Disputes about pay | 0-4 | 5-8 | 9-12 | 13-16 | 17-20 | 21-24 | 25-28 | 29-32 | 33+ | Av. no. per mon |
| 14 | Man hours lost in pay disputes | 0-4 | 5-8 | 9-12 | 13-16 | 17-20 | 21-24 | 25-28 | 29-32 | 33+ | % per mon |
| 15 | % earnings decided outside plant/company | 0-10 | 11-20 | 21-30 | 31-40 | 41-50 | 51-60 | 61-70 | 71-80 | 81+ | % |
| 16 | Number of trade unions | 0 | 1-3 | 4-6 | 7-9 | 10-12 | 13-15 | 16-18 | 19-21 | 22+ | All plan |
| 17 | Occupational structure | 0-3 | 4-6 | 7-9 | 10-12 | 13-15 | 16-18 | 19-21 | 22-24 | 25+ | All plan |
| 18 | Absence | 0 | 2-3 | 4-5 | 6-7 | 8-9 | 10-11 | 12-13 | 14-15 | 16+ | % normal |
| 19 | Average age of working force | 15-29 | | | 30-44 | | | 45+ | | | Years |
| 20 | % labour cost in unit cost | 23+ | 21-23 | 18-20 | 15-17 | 12-14 | 10-12 | 7-9 | 4-6 | 1-3 | % |
| 21 | % males in working force | 0 | to 10 | 11-20 | 21-30 | 31-40 | 41-50 | 51-60 | 61-70 | 71+ | % All plan |

*Figure 16. Component Assembly*

64

mix, material shortages, and constant order variations and modifications meant that management itself was restricted. How far such restriction had been forced upon them by the change in product policy without changing their production facilities is difficult to assess. Flow-line designed plant was attempting to cope with small batch engineering orders, with the associated problems of adapting purpose-built machinery, frequent shortages and increased material handling. The emphasis on labour flexibility (rather than lay-out and plant redesign) in the payment system might have been an adaptation to the 'mismatch' between plant design and their current product policy. In profile terms this probably contributed to some of the profile scores recorded — in particular on (2), (4), (5), (6) and (9).

However, the profile scores obtained in the selected three areas of the firm do not suggest a particularly strong case for an incentive scheme. *The component assembly line* was a small batch line operated by setter operators. Production was continually disrupted by the number of modifications, the high rate of product change and shortages that frequently gave rise to long stoppages on the production line — apparently re-deployment to other work was not possible, or other work not made available by supervision. Management considered that this line was in fact a 'poor example of measured day work'. In part this was said to be due to poor layout design and weak supervision. Labour costs were a relatively high proportion of unit costs. However, here a poor measured day work scheme does not suggest that an incentive scheme is any more appropriate. A reciprocal immediate scheme would still have to deal with profile chacteristics (2), (4), (5) and (6) — at the moment this represents a loss in output at a cost to the firm, rather than a loss in output at the cost of the operatives' earnings (as would occur under an incentive scheme).

*The small part machining line* was manned by both setters and operators. Management considered this to be a 'good measured day work line'. Again this was an integrated line and consequently, although it only experienced a few stoppages, a great deal of time was lost through such stoppages. Management said that this line had adequate stock

| 1(g) Type of effort | Time | | | Energy | | | Competence | | | |
|---|---|---|---|---|---|---|---|---|---|---|
| 2(g) Unit of accountability | Individual | | | Group | | | Plant | | | |
| | 1 | 2 | 3 | 4 | 5 | 6 | 7 | 8 | 9 | |
| 1 Length of job cycle | to 5 | 6-10 | 11-15 | 16-30 | 31-45 | 46-60 | 61-90 | 91-120 | 121+ | Mins. |
| 2. Number of job modifications | 0 | 1 | 2 | 3 | 4 | 5 | 6 | 7 | 8+ | Av. no per m( |
| 3 Degree of automation | SPT | PAT | SMT | CMT | STM | CTM | SPO | CPO | CCP | |
| 4 Number of product changes | 0 | 1 | 2 | 3 | 4 | 5 | 6 | 7 | 8+ | Av. no per m( |
| 5 Number of job stoppages | 0 | 1 | 2 | 3 | 4 | 5 | 6 | 7 | 8+ | Av. no per da |
| 6 Duration of job stoppages | 0 | 1-5 | 6-10 | 11-20 | 21-30 | 31-40 | 41-50 | 51-60 | 61+ | A\ no per da |
| 7 % job elements specified by management | 71+ | 61-70 | 51-60 | 41-50 | 31-40 | 21-30 | 11-20 | 1-10 | 0 | % |
| 8 % material scrapped | 0 | 1-2 | 3-4 | 5-6 | 7-8 | 9-10 | 11-12 | 13-14 | 15+ | % |
| 9 % products/components rejected | 0 | 1-2 | 3-4 | 5-6 | 7-8 | 9-10 | 11-12 | 13-14 | 15+ | % |
| 10 Time required to fill vacancy | 1 | 2-4 | 5-7 | 8-10 | 11-13 | 14-16 | 17-19 | 20-22 | 23+ | Days |
| 11 Labour stability | 81+ | 71-80 | 61-70 | 51-60 | 41-50 | 31-40 | 21-30 | 11-20 | 0-10 | % |
| 12 Labour turnover | 0 / 0 | 6 / 12 | 12 / 24 | 18 / 36 | 24 / 48 | 30 / 60 | 36 / 72 | 42 / 84 | 48 / 96 | Men Wome( |
| 13 Disputes about pay | 0-4 | 5-8 | 9-12 | 13-16 | 17-20 | 21-24 | 25-28 | 29-32 | 33+ | Av. n( per m( |
| 14 Man hours lost in pay disputes | 0-4 | 5-8 | 9-12 | 13-16 | 17-20 | 21-24 | 25-28 | 29-32 | 33+ | % per m( |
| 15 % earnings decided outside plant/company | 0-10 | 11-20 | 21-30 | 31-40 | 41-50 | 51-60 | 61-70 | 71-80 | 81+ | % |
| 16 Number of trade unions | 0 | 1-3 | 4-6 | 7-9 | 10-12 | 13-15 | 16-18 | 19-21 | 22+ | All pla |
| 17 Occupational structure | 0-3 | 4-6 | 7-9 | 10-12 | 13-15 | 16-18 | 19-21 | 22-24 | 25+ | All pla |
| 18 Absence | 0 | 2-3 | 4-5 | 6-7 | 8-9 | 10-11 | 12-13 | 14-15 | 16+ | % norma |
| 19 Average age of working force | 15-29 | | | 30-44 | | | 45+ | | | Years |
| 20 % labour cost in unit cost | 23+ | 21-23 | 18-20 | 15-17 | 12-14 | 10-12 | 7-9 | 4-6 | 1-3 | % |
| 21 % males in working force | 0 | to 10 | 11-20 | 21-30 | 31-40 | 41-50 | 51-60 | 61-70 | 71+ | % All pla |

*Figure 17. Small Part Machining Line*

| (g) | Type of effort | Time | | | Energy | | | Competence | | | |
|---|---|---|---|---|---|---|---|---|---|---|---|
| (g) | Unit of accountability | Individual | | | Group | | | Plant | | | |
| | | 1 | 2 | 3 | 4 | 5 | 6 | 7 | 8 | 9 | |
| | Length of job cycle | to 5 | 6-10 | 11-15 | 16-30 | 31-45 | 46-60 | 61-90 | 91-120 | 121+ | Mins. |
| | Number of job modifications | 0 | 1 | 2 | 3 | 4 | 5 | 6 | 7 | 8+ | Av. no. per month |
| | Degree of automation | SPT | PAT | SMT | GMT | STM | CTM | SPO | CPO | CCP | |
| | Number of product changes | 0 | 1 | 2 | 3 | 4 | 5 | 6 | 7 | 8+ | Av. no. per month |
| | Number of job stoppages | 0 | 1 | 2 | 3 | 4 | 5 | 6 | 7 | 8+ | Av. no. per day |
| | Duration of job stoppages | 0 | 1-5 | 6-10 | 11-20 | 21-30 | 31-40 | 41-50 | 51-60 | 61+ | Av. no. mins. per day |
| | % job elements specified by management | 71+ | 61-70 | 51-60 | 41-50 | 31-40 | 21-30 | 11-20 | 1-10 | 0 | % |
| | % material scrapped | 0 | 1-2 | 3-4 | 5-6 | 7-8 | 9-10 | 11-12 | 13-14 | 15+ | % |
| | % products/components rejected | 0 | 1-2 | 3-4 | 5-6 | 7-8 | 9-10 | 11-12 | 13-14 | 15+ | % |
| | Time required to fill vacancy | 1 | 2-4 | 5-7 | 8-10 | 11-13 | 14-16 | 17-19 | 20-22 | 23+ | Days |
| | Labour stability | 81+ | 71-80 | 61-70 | 51-60 | 41-50 | 31-40 | 21-30 | 11-20 | 0-10 | % |
| | Labour turnover | 0 | 6 | 12 | 18 | 24 | 30 | 36 | 42 | 48 | Men % |
| | | 0 | 12 | 24 | 36 | 48 | 60 | 72 | 84 | 96 | Women % |
| | Disputes about pay | 0-4 | 5-8 | 9-12 | 13-16 | 17-20 | 21-24 | 25-28 | 29-32 | 33+ | Av. no. per month |
| | Man hours lost in pay disputes | 0-4 | 5-8 | 9-12 | 13-16 | 17-20 | 21-24 | 25-28 | 29-32 | 33+ | % per month |
| | % earnings decided outside plant/company | 0-10 | 11-20 | 21-30 | 31-40 | 41-50 | 51-60 | 61-70 | 71-80 | 81+ | % |
| | Number of trade unions | 0 | 1-3 | 4-6 | 7-9 | 10-12 | 13-15 | 16-18 | 19-21 | 22+ | All plant |
| | Occupational structure | 0-3 | 4-6 | 7-9 | 10-12 | 13-15 | 16-18 | 19-21 | 22-24 | 25+ | All plant |
| | Absence | 0 | 2-3 | 4-5 | 6-7 | 8-9 | 10-11 | 12-13 | 14-15 | 16+ | % normal hours |
| | Average age of working force | 15-29 | | | 30-44 | | | 45+ | | | Years |
| | % labour cost in unit cost | 23+ | 21-23 | 18-20 | 15-17 | 12-14 | 10-12 | 7-9 | 4-6 | 1-3 | % |
| | % males in working force | 0 | to 10 | 11-20 | 21-30 | 31-40 | 41-50 | 51-60 | 61-70 | 71+ | % All plant |

*Figure 18.* Heavy Machining Flow Line

levels throughout its length and a lower rate of product change than the other lines. These 'dimensional' differences probably contributed to the better operator performances obtained — though dimensions (6), (9), and (12) are 'misfits'. The opinion of the work study officer on a 'good measured day work' line appears to coincide with that which had the lowest non-reciprocal score of all the areas analysed. This needs to be compared with the findings on the measured day work scheme in firm B which had a more developed supervisory structure.

On *the heavy machining flow line* the machines were automatic and purpose built — this was said to compensate for weak supervision in this area. Stoppages were few and the rate of product change low, but as the line was integrated total 'down-time' was again high, due to the characteristics of the technology. To increase output from this line, management were now working shifts, though the profile suggests that there might be scope for increasing output if some of the profile dimensions of the situation could be improved.

On the basis of the current scoring the small part machining line is the nearest 'fit' to an incentive situation, i.e. the line that was regarded as the best measured day work line.[9]

The firm's future plans included:


1. Introducing a completely new product into the plant
2. Introducing a planned maintenance scheme
3. Expanding production capacity
4. Introducing a computer-based material movement system.


All these changes were expected to be accompanied by a large injection of new labour. In the light of these changes it was suggested that a change in their payment method might be better after such changes rather than before, as the incentive scheme would probably be more sensitive to such

[9] See revisions to Lupton-Gowler logic p.90-101

changes than their current scheme. This would also depend on an assessment of how far management could satisfactorily manage such innovation in their production areas. It must be recalled that they were experiencing difficulties at the moment — some of which might be unresolved because of supplies and product mix constraints.

## Conclusion for Non-Financial Rewards Ltd.

Some of the current difficulties of their payment system might have arisen from the changes in the firm's product policy which had not been matched by changes in basic plant design. The implications of such changes in management objectives had not been fully worked through on the shop floor. The frequent failure to meet output targets and the erosion of 'standards' could in part be attributed to the mismatch of product policy and production facilities.

The weakness in the effort bargain under the current payment scheme was also attributed to inadequate supervision, in addition to the restrictions of the work situation. Foremen were blamed for 'fiddling' production reports though it was recognised that such foremen's behaviour was not of equal importance in all of the production areas of the firm — for example it was recognised as being less important on the heavy machining line. Such weakness in supervision might have been attributed to the effect of the labour market constraints; supervision might have in fact been accepting less 'effort' in order to retain labour in a tight labour market. Some weaknesses in their current scheme, however, might have been due to the administrative basis of their particular form of measured day work. The monitoring of the 'effort' component in this firm is recorded as 'group' (see firm B). In each of the areas, reports and records were kept based on 'line performance' — not individual performances. This would have further obscured the relationship between effort and reward, and the establishment of the effort bargain with their fixed reward structure. The measured day work scheme might have been more effective if it had been changed to individual accountability from group accountability. Consequently one might then query the accuracy of the percentage of job elements specified by management in this situation.

Though the pay packet was relatively fixed, additional payment could be added to the basic consolidated rate by obtaining a 'leading hand' allowance, being up-graded in the current grade structure (if high labour turnover required redeployment there was a built-in opportunity to be upgraded), undertaking shift work to obtain shift premiums or by working overtime. Overtime represented over twenty per cent of the total hours worked in all of the areas analysed. Alternatively, although earnings might remain the same the pay packet might be more attractive were 'effort' to be less — which was the type of adjustment that management was now criticising the supervisory staff for having made, i.e. lowering or obscuring 'standards'. The suggested re-structuring of the payment method to an incentive pay packet in these restricted situations would *not* have solved some of their payment problems. With an incentive type of scheme most of the 'misfit' dimensions would require the payment of 'allowances' or substantial adminstrative work by supervision in an attempt to minimise the impact of the situational factors. As supervisory influence is currently limited in some areas, for example on the heavy machining lines, there might be little scope for improved supervisory 'efforts' and consequently non-output related allowances might form a significant part of the operatives' so-called incentive pay packet.

Currently, the restricted nature of the situation and supervision's failure to maintain 'effort' might mean that the scheme had in effect changed to a 'time' scheme. Even with the payment of high levels of overtime this addition was apparently insufficient to retain labour and combat the labour market constraint. If management pay out to insulate themselves from the labour market pressures rather than introduce an incentive they might regain control of their pay scheme by improving the supervisor's authority to sustain the 'effort' bargain under their payment method. Although an incentive scheme in this situation might facilitate higher earnings — and so protect the firm from the labour market —

this would also be accompanied by substantial administrative costs of running such a scheme in their situation. In addition however, the introduction of an incentive scheme to some of the areas of the firm might not automatically facilitate an increase in earnings as some of the situational characteristics are likely to restrict operator effort rather than facilitate the achievement of incentive earnings.

It might be worth mentioning the implications of the other alternative rewards considered by management as a substitute for paying out i.e. job enrichment, job satisfaction, increased job security and staff status. In Lupton-Gowler terms job enrichment and satisfaction, if applied to the current labour force, means an increase in the length of the job cycle, greater operator skill and flexibility and increased training times (and costs). First, it might be asked how far such profile changes would be feasible with the current technology and product market characteristics; and if feasible, how far it would actually increase output? The provision of job security in this firm may have been important had the labour market situation been poor from the operatives' point of view. However, the current high level of labour turnover which here indicated the availability of alternative job opportunities would probably have meant that the provision of job security would not have been very effective, as job security was currently assured by the state of the labour market. Again, one might ask about the feasibility and costs of such rewards, — can the firm avoid redundancies, could it afford the training costs, and costs of having trainees if new skills were required, would the provision of security mean that the firm would have an ageing labour force? The provision of staff status would affect the traditional staff and non-staff differential and if staff and non-staff conditions or working arrangements are dissimilar the need for differential payments might still arise. *From the profile diagnosis it would appear to be unlikely that any of these simple alternatives in themselves would regain management's control of the payment system in the areas of firm C that were investigated.*

## (D) Management-Union Agreement Ltd.

**Payment problems? There are no problems as both top management and senior union officials are in agreement over the methods of payment and the wage structure of the firm.**

It was decided to examine the firm's payment methods as a contribution to a productivity improvement programme that was currently being undertaken. The areas assessed were then subjected to detailed examination for productivity improvement. In this firm a strong time-study work measurement tradition existed and most of the schemes were of the incentive type (here known as 'direct system'). The appropriateness of these methods of payment was subject to a great deal of discussion between those who decided the rules on payment and those who had to work with them. Union agreements, payment methods and the wage structure were formulated and negotiated centrally and the management of the payment system was seen as applying and obtaining conformity to the centrally agreed payment rules, procedures and rates.

As it was possible to discuss the method of payment, and the particular situation to which it was applied, with each departmental manager, the manager's description of his payment problems is taken as the central theme in this account of profile analysis.

The following areas were covered with the objective of examining the scope for improved productivity:

1. Grinding and Polishing Department
2. Diverse Press Department
3. Special Hot Press Department
4. Melting Department

Although profile analysis was undertaken at both the departmental and job-group level within the department — to examine the most useful level of analysis — space does not permit the detailed discussion of these findings here.

72

### Grinding and Polishing Department

This department was working at full capacity on a three shift system and operators were paid on an incentive basis. From the recorded scores it appears that for the department as a whole and for the majority of the work groups the incentive method of payment is appropriate — though the polisher's particular profile is less compatible with an incentive method of payment.

**Profile Scores — Grinding and Polishing**

|  | Effort | Accountability | RI | RD | NR |  |
|---|---|---|---|---|---|---|
| Department | Energy | Group | 36 | 10 | (6) | 12 |
| Separate (Servicemen ( (Grinders | Energy | Group | 35 | 14 | (6) | 12 |
| Job ( | Energy | Group | 34 | 11 | (7) | 14 |
| Groups (Checker ( | Energy | Group | 46 | 3 | (8) | 16 |
| (Polishers | Energy | Group | 28 | 6 | (13) | 26 |

Although the current profile situation suggests that an incentive fit is appropriate, the departmental manager's comments revealed that the current situation may well be atypical. The area was subject to significant changes. He pointed out that although production had been running at capacity over the last six months there were usually large fluctuations in product demand and such variations in demand required different patterns of shift-working, manning and different ratios of operators. These fluctuations gave rise to bottlenecks in production which did not contribute to high labour performances and had led to 'inequities' in earnings. All such changes would radically alter the current profile pattern. In the current situation the main bottleneck in production existed on the polishers' job. This had created 'inequities' in earnings and the labour turnover of this job

| | | | | Time | | | Energy | | | Competence | | | |
|---|---|---|---|---|---|---|---|---|---|---|---|---|---|
| 1(g) | Type of effort | | | Time | | | Energy | | | Competence | | | |
| 2(g) | Unit of accountability | | | Individual | | | Group | | | Plant | | | |
| | | | | 1 | 2 | 3 | 4 | 5 | 6 | 7 | 8 | 9 | |
| 1 | Length of job cycle | | | to 5 | 6-10 | 11-15 | 16-30 | 31-45 | 46-60 | 61-90 | 91-120 | 121+ | Mins. |
| 2 | Number of job modifications | | | 0 | 1 | 2 | 3 | 4 | 5 | 6 | 7 | 8+ | Av. no. per month |
| 3 | Degree of automation | | | SFT | PAT | SMT | CMT | STM | CTM | SPO | CPO | CCP | |
| 4 | Number of product changes | | | 0 | 1 | 2 | 3 | 4 | 5 | 6 | 7 | 8+ | Av. no. per month |
| 5 | Number of job stoppages | | | 0 | 1 | 2 | 3 | 4 | 5 | 6 | 7 | 8+ | Av. no. per day |
| 6 | Duration of job stoppages | | | 0 | 1-5 | 6-10 | 11-20 | 21-30 | 31-40 | 41-50 | 51-60 | 61+ | Av. no. m per day |
| 7 | % job elements specified by management | | | 71+ | 61-70 | 51-60 | 41-50 | 31-40 | 21-30 | 11-20 | 1-10 | 0 | % |
| 8 | % material scrapped | | | 0 | 1-2 | 3-4 | 5-6 | 7-8 | 9-10 | 11-12 | 13-14 | 15+ | % |
| 9 | % products/components rejected | | | 0 | 1-2 | 3-4 | 5-6 | 7-8 | 9-10 | 11-12 | 13-14 | 15+ | % |
| 10 | Time required to fill vacancy | | | 1 | 2-4 | 5-7 | 8-10 | 11-13 | 14-16 | 17-19 | 20-22 | 23+ | Days |
| 11 | Labour stability | | | 81+ | 71-80 | 61-70 | 51-60 | 41-50 | 31-40 | 21-30 | 11-20 | 0-10 | % |
| 12 | Labour turnover | | | 0 / 0 | 6 / 12 | 12 / 24 | 18 / 36 | 24 / 48 | 30 / 60 | 36 / 72 | 42 / 84 | 48 / 96 | Men / Women |
| 13 | Disputes about pay | | | 0-4 | 5-8 | 9-12 | 13-16 | 17-20 | 21-24 | 25-28 | 29-32 | 33+ | Av. no. per month |
| 14 | Man hours lost in pay disputes | | | 0-4 | 5-8 | 9-12 | 13-16 | 17-20 | 21-24 | 25-28 | 29-32 | 33+ | % per month |
| 15 | % earnings decided outside plant/company | | | 0-10 | 11-20 | 21-30 | 31-40 | 41-50 | 51-60 | 61-70 | 71-80 | 81+ | % |
| 16 | Number of trade unions | | | 0 | 1-3 | 4-6 | 7-9 | 10-12 | 13-15 | 16-18 | 19-21 | 22+ | All plant |
| 17 | Occupational structure | | | 0-3 | 4-6 | 7-9 | 10-12 | 13-15 | 16-18 | 19-21 | 22-24 | 25+ | All plant |
| 18 | Absence | | | 0 | 2-3 | 4-5 | 6-7 | 8-9 | 10-11 | 12-13 | 14-15 | 16+ | % normal h |
| 19 | Average age of working force | | | 15-29 | | | 30-44 | | | 45+ | | | Years |
| 20 | % labour cost in unit cost | | | 23+ | 21-23 | 18-20 | 15-17 | 12-14 | 10-12 | 7-9 | 4-6 | 1-3 | % |
| 21 | % males in working force | | | 0 | to 10 | 11-20 | 21-30 | 31-40 | 41-50 | 51-60 | 61-70 | 71+ | % All plant |

*Figure 19. Grinding and Polishing*

74

group was high. The bottlenecks in production and 'inequities' in earnings probably changed with the different levels of output and consequently the effectiveness of the scheme might well have changed with the different levels of output.

An examination of the completed profile of this department shows that the scores (1) to (15) and (18) to (20), which represent the particular work characteristics *within* the area, differ from the profile scores of dimensions (16), (17) and (21) — the all-plant dimensions. The latter scores indicate that an incentive scheme *within* the area is appropriate, though the non-reciprocal scores *outside* the area suggest that the method of payment might be particularly vulnerable to *differential disputes* from the firm's complex occupational structure.

### Special Hot Press Department.
Again, incentive schemes were the most common method of payment in this department, and most tended to be of the individual or small group type. The manager of the department said that the major problem in this area was the re-deployment of labour and described the situation as 'a continual battle over the movement of personnel'.

Though the work technology and the product mix variations required the continual re-deployment of personnel, the payment system in this situation was considered to be a barrier to such movement. This was said to be primarily due to the fact that when operators were transferred from one 'incentive situation' to another operatives lost earnings, as there were no guarantees or allowances given to compensate for the effect of being re-deployed. The deployment problem was probably made more acute by widespread earnings instability in many parts of this department. The manager said that earnings were often erratic (though on an average over six months they would be fairly constant!) due to the characteristics of the technology and the incidence of machine breakdown (which often required transferring labour). This frequently reduced operatives' levels of bonus earnings even though such factors were beyond their control and 'efforts'. This reinforced the anxiety of re-deployment.

## Profile Scores — Special Hot Press

| | Effort | Accountability | R.I. | R.D. | N.R. |
|---|---|---|---|---|---|
| Department | | | 18 | 14 | 20 (40) |
| Machine Hand | | | 31 | 14 | 12 (24) |
| Operator | | | 23 | 9 | 24 (48) |
| Cleaner | | Individual | 34 | 4 | 18 (36) |
| Hot Sorter | Energy | & | 25 | 6 | 22 (44) |
| Adjuster | | Group | 35 | 10 | 9 (18) |
| Gauger | | | 26 | 3 | 24 (48) |
| Chargehand Operator | | | 21 | 8 | 24 (48) |

He also commented that reward differentials were insufficient to retain the better operatives on the particular types of work where they were most useful. This under-utilised the better operative and overstretched the poorer operatives. The inappropriate method of payment and the resultant pay structure substantially contributed to a loss of control over output in a work situation that required it.

The high non-reciprocal scores recorded and the profile pattern of the department seem to bear out some of the manager's comments on the appropriateness of their payment methods and the resultant loss of managerial control through the application of incentive payment rules in a complex and dynamic situation.

### Diverse Press Department.

Though the completed profile of the department has a high non-reciprocal score the analysis of several of the job groups reveals that some do not show as high a non-reciprocal score: this suggests that the situation's characteristics vary a great

76

| Type of effort | Time | | | Energy | | | Competence | | | |
|---|---|---|---|---|---|---|---|---|---|---|
| Unit of accountability | Individual | | | Group | | | Plant | | | |
| | 1 | 2 | 3 | 4 | 5 | 6 | 7 | 8 | 9 | |
| Length of job cycle | to 5 | 6-10 | 11-15 | 16-30 | 31-45 | 46-60 | 61-90 | 91-120 | 121+ | Mins. |
| Number of job modifications | 0 | 1 | 2 | 3 | 4 | 5 | 6 | 7 | 8+ | Av. no. per month |
| Degree of automation | SPT | PAT | SMT | CMT | STM | CTM | SPO | CPO | CCP | |
| Number of product changes | 0 | 1 | 2 | 3 | 4 | 5 | 6 | 7 | 8+ | Av. no. per month |
| Number of job stoppages | 0 | 1 | 2 | 3 | 4 | 5 | 6 | 7 | 8+ | Av. no. per day |
| Duration of job stoppages | 0 | 1-5 | 6-10 | 11-20 | 21-30 | 31-40 | 41-50 | 51-60 | 61+ | Av. no. mins. per day |
| % job elements specified by management | 71+ | 61-70 | 51-60 | 41-50 | 31-40 | 21-30 | 11-20 | 1-10 | 0 | % |
| % material scrapped | 0 | 1-2 | 3-4 | 5-6 | 7-8 | 9-10 | 11-12 | 13-14 | 15+ | % |
| % products/components rejected | 0 | 1-2 | 3-4 | 5-6 | 7-8 | 9-10 | 11-12 | 13-14 | 15+ | % |
| Time required to fill vacancy | 1 | 2-4 | 5-7 | 8-10 | 11-13 | 14-16 | 17-19 | 20-22 | 23+ | Days |
| Labour stability | 81+ | 71-80 | 61-70 | 51-60 | 41-50 | 31-40 | 21-30 | 11-20 | 0-10 | % |
| Labour turnover | 0 / 0 | 6 / 12 | 12 / 24 | 18 / 36 | 24 / 48 | 30 / 60 | 36 / 72 | 42 / 84 | 48 / 96 | Men % / Women % |
| Disputes about pay | 0-4 | 5-8 | 9-12 | 13-16 | 17-20 | 21-24 | 25-28 | 29-32 | 33+ | Av. no. per month |
| Man hours lost in pay disputes | 0-4 | 5-8 | 9-12 | 13-16 | 17-20 | 21-24 | 25-28 | 29-32 | 33+ | % per month |
| % earnings decided outside plant/company | 0-10 | 11-20 | 21-30 | 31-40 | 41-50 | 51-60 | 61-70 | 71-80 | 81+ | % |
| Number of trade unions | 0 | 1-3 | 4-6 | 7-9 | 10-12 | 13-15 | 16-18 | 19-21 | 22+ | All plant |
| Occupational structure | 0-3 | 4-6 | 7-9 | 10-12 | 13-15 | 16-18 | 19-21 | 22-24 | 25+ | All plant |
| Absence | 0 | 2-3 | 4-5 | 6-7 | 8-9 | 10-11 | 12-13 | 14-15 | 16+ | % normal hours |
| Average age of working force | 15-29 | | | 30-44 | | | 45+ | | | Years |
| % labour cost in unit cost | 23+ | 21-23 | 18-20 | 15-17 | 12-14 | 10-12 | 7-9 | 4-6 | 1-3 | % |
| % males in working force | 0 | to 10 | 11-20 | 21-30 | 31-40 | 41-50 | 51-60 | 61-70 | 71+ | % All plant |

*Figure 20. Special Hot Press Department*

deal within this selected area. The manager's general comments might then be expected to be less representive of the general situation than they were in the previous area.

Profile Scores — Diverse Press

|  | Effort | Accountability | RI | RD | NR |
|---|---|---|---|---|---|
| Department |  |  | 17 | 13 | 20 (40) |
| Tougheners (Auto) |  |  | 31 | 5 | 12 (24) |
| (Hand) |  |  | 26 | 4 | 18 (36) |
| Supplier |  |  | 29 | 12 | 9 (18) |
| Assistant Supplier |  | Individual | 26 | 11 | 13 (26) |
| Skilled Operator |  | & | 25 | 15 | 9 (18) |
| Hot Sorter | Energy |  | 30 | 8 | 11 (22) |
| Foreheath Attendant |  | Group | 33 | 5 | 17 (34) |
| Operator |  |  | 23 | 11 | 22 (44) |
| Waste Man |  |  | 32 | 5 | 15 (30) |
| Assistant |  |  | 30 | 6 | 11 (22) |
| Machine Hand |  |  | 28 | 16 | 15 (30) |

Again, the manager mentioned the 'labour flexibility' problem and said that it was not only an inherent source of conflict but also the most frequent subject of dispute between men and management. The manager said that their major flexibility problems were on the presses — most of the incentive schemes were designed on an individual or small group basis for each press. Essentially there were two types of presses in the department — the automatic and hand (the

78

| | Time | | | Energy | | | Competence | | | |
|---|---|---|---|---|---|---|---|---|---|---|
| (g) Type of effort | | | | | | | | | | |
| (g) Unit of accountability | Individual | | | Group | | | Plant | | | |
| | 1 | 2 | 3 | 4 | 5 | 6 | 7 | 8 | 9 | |
| 1 Length of job cycle | to 5 | 6-10 | 11-15 | 16-30 | 31-45 | 46-60 | 61-90 | 91-120 | 121+ | Mins. |
| 2 Number of job modifications | 0 | 1 | 2 | 3 | 4 | 5 | 6 | 7 | 8+ | Av. no. per month |
| 3 Degree of automation | SPT | PAT | SMT | CMT | STM | CTM | SPO | CPO | CCP | |
| 4 Number of product changes | 0 | 1 | 2 | 3 | 4 | 5 | 6 | 7 | 8+ | Av. no. per month |
| 5 Number of job stoppages | 0 | 1 | 2 | 3 | 4 | 5 | 6 | 7 | 8+ | Av. no. per day |
| 6 Duration of job stoppages | 0 | 1-5 | 6-10 | 11-20 | 21-30 | 31-40 | 41-50 | 51-60 | 61+ | Av. no. mins. per day |
| 7 % job elements specified by management | 71+ | 61-70 | 51-60 | 41-50 | 31-40 | 21-30 | 11-20 | 1-10 | 0 | % |
| 8 % material scrapped | 0 | 1-2 | 3-4 | 5-6 | 7-8 | 9-10 | 11-12 | 13-14 | 15+ | % |
| 9 % products/components rejected | 0 | 1-2 | 3-4 | 5-6 | 7-8 | 9-10 | 11-12 | 13-14 | 15+ | % |
| 10 Time required to fill vacancy | 1 | 2-4 | 5-7 | 8-10 | 11-13 | 14-16 | 17-19 | 20-22 | 23+ | Days |
| 11 Labour stability | 81+ | 71-80 | 61-70 | 51-60 | 41-50 | 31-40 | 21-30 | 11-20 | 0-10 | % |
| 12 Labour turnover | 0 / 0 | 6 / 12 | 12 / 24 | 18 / 36 | 24 / 48 | 30 / 60 | 36 / 72 | 42 / 84 | 48 / 96 | Men % / Women % |
| 13 Disputes about pay | 0-4 | 5-8 | 9-12 | 13-16 | 17-20 | 21-24 | 25-28 | 29-32 | 33+ | Av. no. per month |
| 14 Man hours lost in pay disputes | 0-4 | 5-8 | 9-12 | 13-16 | 17-20 | 21-24 | 25-28 | 29-32 | 33+ | % per month |
| 15 % earnings decided outside plant/company | 0-10 | 11-20 | 21-30 | 31-40 | 41-50 | 51-60 | 61-70 | 71-80 | 81+ | % |
| 16 Number of trade unions | 0 | 1-3 | 4-6 | 7-9 | 10-12 | 13-15 | 16-18 | 19-21 | 22+ | All plant |
| 17 Occupational structure | 0-3 | 4-6 | 7-9 | 10-12 | 13-15 | 16-18 | 19-21 | 22-24 | 25+ | All plant |
| 18 Absence | 0 | 2-3 | 4-5 | 6-7 | 8-9 | 10-11 | 12-13 | 14-15 | 16+ | % normal hours |
| 19 Average age of working force | 15-29 | | | 30-44 | | | 45+ | | | Years |
| 20 % labour cost in unit cost | 23+ | 21-23 | 18-20 | 15-17 | 12-14 | 10-12 | 7-9 | 4-6 | 1-3 | % |
| 21 % males in working force | 0 | to 10 | 11-20 | 21-30 | 31-40 | 41-50 | 51-60 | 61-70 | 71+ | % All plant |

*Figure 21. Diverse Press Department*

most numerous) presses. Usually large batches were produced on the automatic presses and the smaller batches on the hand presses. As the department dealt with such a wide range of items, stock often did not exist for many items or was low for the less frequently demanded items. Consequently, to meet orders flexibility was a constant production requirement on the hand presses. But here operatives lacking experience of the particular types of presses and the vast range of product and press combinations often lost earnings when they were transferred between the presses. Local management had attempted to pay them 'average' but work study insisted that operatives be paid the fixed incentive rate for the work. Until recently the hand press operators had also been penalised for high reject rates (which might be expected to be a consequence of the effect of redeployment and the small batch size produced) under the incentive pay rules. This had reinforced their particular deployment problem, but now, after a great deal of discussion with the work study officers the manager was able to use his discretion on payment when rejected items were produced. This removed some of the tension that had previously been generated by redeployment between the hand presses. However, payment problems were not solely restricted to the hand presses; the automatic press operatives also disputed the immediate and significant impact of their 'bonus' earnings that occurred when the automatic press machines broke down — again no payment allowance was give for such breakdowns and operatives were expected to bear the cost of such events via a loss in 'bonus' earnings.

The manager concluded by saying that the incentive payment methods created difficulty in managing the department and this was not improved by work study's insistence on rigidly interpreting the management and the union agreements on payment.

### Melting Department
Discussing the characteristics of the profiled situation, the manager mentioned that the quality variation of both the raw and processed material produced in this department created payment problems for most of the other departments. The

| Type of effort | Time | | | Energy | | | Competence | | | |
|---|---|---|---|---|---|---|---|---|---|---|
| Unit of accountability | Individual | | | Group | | | Plant | | | |
| | 1 | 2 | 3 | 4 | 5 | 6 | 7 | 8 | 9 | |
| Length of job cycle | to 5 | 6-10 | 11-15 | 16-30 | 31-45 | 46-60 | 61-90 | 91-120 | 121+ | Mins. |
| Number of job modifications | 0 | 1 | 2 | 3 | 4 | 5 | 6 | 7 | 8+ | Av. no. per month |
| Degree of automation | SPT | PAT | SMT | CMT | STM | CTM | SPO | CPO | CCP | |
| Number of product changes | 0 | 1 | 2 | 3 | 4 | 5 | 6 | 7 | 8+ | Av. no. per month |
| Number of job stoppages | 0 | 1 | 2 | 3 | 4 | 5 | 6 | 7 | 8+ | Av. no. per day |
| Duration of job stoppages | 0 | 1-5 | 6-10 | 11-20 | 21-30 | 31-40 | 41-50 | 51-60 | 61+ | Av. no. mins. per day |
| % job elements specified by management | 71+ | 61-70 | 51-60 | 41-50 | 31-40 | 21-30 | 11-20 | 1-10 | 0 | % |
| % material scrapped | 0 | 1-2 | 3-4 | 5-6 | 7-8 | 9-10 | 11-12 | 13-14 | 15+ | % |
| % products/components rejected | 0 | 1-2 | 3-4 | 5-6 | 7-8 | 9-10 | 11-12 | 13-14 | 15+ | % |
| Time required to fill vacancy | 1 | 2-4 | 5-7 | 8-10 | 11-13 | 14-16 | 17-19 | 20-22 | 23+ | Days |
| Labour stability | 81+ | 71-80 | 61-70 | 51-60 | 41-50 | 31-40 | 21-30 | 11-20 | 0-10 | % |
| Labour turnover | 0 | 6 | 12 | 18 | 24 | 30 | 36 | 42 | 48 | Men % |
| | 0 | 12 | 24 | 36 | 48 | 60 | 72 | 84 | 96 | Women % |
| Disputes about pay | 0-4 | 5-8 | 9-12 | 13-16 | 17-20 | 21-24 | 25-28 | 29-32 | 33+ | Av. no. per month |
| Man hours lost in pay disputes | 0-4 | 5-8 | 9-12 | 13-16 | 17-20 | 21-24 | 25-28 | 29-32 | 33+ | % per month |
| % earnings decided outside plant/company | 0-10 | 11-20 | 21-30 | 31-40 | 41-50 | 51-60 | 61-70 | 71-80 | 81+ | % |
| Number of trade unions | 0 | 1-3 | 4-6 | 7-9 | 10-12 | 13-15 | 16-18 | 19-21 | 22+ | All plant |
| Occupational structure | 0-3 | 4-6 | 7-9 | 10-12 | 13-15 | 16-18 | 19-21 | 22-24 | 25+ | All plant |
| Absence | 0 | 2-3 | 4-5 | 6-7 | 8-9 | 10-11 | 12-13 | 14-15 | 16+ | % normal hours |
| Average age of working force | 15-29 | | | 30-44 | | | 45+ | | | Years |
| % labour cost in unit cost | 23+ | 21-23 | 18-20 | 15-17 | 12-14 | 10-12 | 7-9 | 4-6 | 1-3 | % |
| % males in working force | 0 | to 10 | 11-20 | 21-30 | 31-40 | 41-50 | 51-60 | 61-70 | 71+ | % All plant |

Figure 22. Melting Department

high scrap rates and reject rates which influenced the bonus schemes (and hence earning levels) were in part due to management's limited technological understanding of the process. The erratic movement of levels of payment was a characteristic of many of the bonus schemes, quite apart from the uncertainty surrounding earning levels when employees were redeployed. He also mentioned that the periodic closure of the plant (necessitated by the nature of the process but also due to inadequate decisions about plant capacity and the product market) required periodic redundancy, transfers and a significant drop in earnings for most of the operatives on incentive payment. As the profile analysis did not take account of major dimensional changes beyond the six month time basis on which it was completed, it is necessary to note the widespread implications that such changes would have on the profile.

Here the scores of the individual job groups are markedly different from the scores of the melting department, i.e. by treating the individual as the unit of production the profile pattern would be different from what it would be by relating it to the wider technological background of the department (unlike the grinding and polishing department). The periodic breakdowns or the occasional production of poor quality material in this department would radically change some of the situational dimensions at the individual level of analysis, consequently such variability of some of the dimensions made the profile even more dynamic than is currently recorded.

### Profile Scores — Melting Department

|  | Effort | Accountability | RI | RD | NR |
|---|---|---|---|---|---|
| Department |  |  | 16 | 7 | 27 (52) |
| Fork Lift Truck Drivers | Energy | Individual | 32 | 1 | 16 (32) |
| First Hand |  |  | 33 | 2 | 15 (30) |
| Cleaners |  |  | 40 | 4 | 15 (30) |

## Conclusion for Management-Union Agreement Ltd.

The current payment system was in many aspects out of the control of local management and in certain areas the method adopted was so dependent on variations in quality, volume and technology that it was out of the control of operatives, supervision and work study! The firm's payment system then had an independent existence which disrupted and restricted production. Occasions arose when for managerial reasons men were transferred and their earnings significantly lowered. This frustrated the manager, the foreman and the men, and at the same time caused a sense of injustice among the men who suffered a loss of earnings as a result. In effect, attempting to transfer men was one way of making them leave, in addition to the labour turnover generated by the unstable earning levels of incentive payment in their situation. Little discretion was given to the manager or foreman in rewarding their men although production expectations were supposed to be met. In all the areas analysed there were large fluctuations in manning levels and these variations were adjusted with different working patterns ranging from day-work to three shift working. The necessity to redeploy large sections of the labour force and the constant changing of work groups, together with the high product mix, the impact of process operations, material quality variations and machine breakdowns, were some of the characteristics that were not appropriate to the piecemeal application of individual and small group incentive schemes.

Most of the departments in this firm suffered from an apparent shortage of personnel. However, this shortage was not related to obtaining personnel, but retaining them with the current pay system — 'we can't keep hold of them', 'they usually come for a few days then leave'. The levels of absenteeism and labour turnover were high throughout the firm, and consequently this reinforced the requirement for further redeployment which generated further labour turnover and absenteeism. If it had been possible to improve the process and quality control aspects of the technology and develop more appropriate product and labour strategies, the incentive schemes would have been more effective. It is

83

surprising that dimensions (13) and (14) do not score more highly. This is not because the consultative and dispute procedures were excellent, but because both the union and management agreed on their methods of payment and the detailed administration of the schemes. In this situation conflict manifested itself in high labour turnover and absenteeism.

Management's reaction to being criticised on the effectiveness of their current pay schemes was to claim that 'work values' had become 'slack'. This frame of reference solved *all* payment problems by retiming, which usually involved tightening the slack values, requiring a more than proportionate increase in effort for the pay currently earned — not a popular activity! The tightening of slack work values was not as frequent an activity as one might have expected in this situation and usually took place in response to individuals or groups achieving high earnings. The occupational structure score indicates that this might have initiated chaos throughout the pay structure. However, inappropriate incentive methods of payment might also have resulted in low earnings though these were not perceived by management as a problem. It was probably easier for management to rationalise their beliefs about the soundness of their 'values' or grade structure with the low pay groups than with the high earning groups (of course, dissatisfied employees usually left). Others who complained about the method of payment, i.e. local management and supervisors, were usually classified as 'trouble-makers'. It is probably true to say that substantial slackness had been built into many of the incentive schemes in order to obtain and maintain production in many of these areas. This was evidenced by the fact that management often commented that at the end of the day 'the men were waiting to go home' or 'finished early' which suggests to the writer that the 'energy' scheme had in fact degenerated into a 'time' scheme with no adaptation on the part of supervision or management to manage the different type of effort-reward relationship. The firm's fixed rulings on payment then also tended to constrain supervisory and managerial behaviour to improve their situation.

Management's discussion on the appropriateness of the

84

firm's payment schemes gave rise to statements such as 'management believed in it' (an act of faith); 'I like the idea of X' (what is liked is right!); or 'they are putting in incentives in other areas' (togetherness?). On balance, views tend to be more concerned with management preferences than with an assessment of the consequent effects of these on employee behaviour, or with the requirements of the immediate management, or with an analysis of the situational influences it might have to adapt to or come into conflict with — though an assessment of these factors was immediately at hand.

Visits to other firms were arranged to discuss the 'current fashions' and it appeared at one stage that the outcome would depend on a general consensus of preferences, rather than an assessment of the requirements of *their* current situation. Current practice in most of the production areas was not so much a question of evaluating payment schemes and supervisory and managerial organisation in the areas but of the piecemeal installation and maintenance of various forms of incentive schemes. The high non-reciprocal scores in most areas suggest that consolidated payment (based on 'time', 'energy' or 'skill') would have been more appropriate in general though there was still scope for incentives in some areas, for example the grinding and polishing department.

In conclusion, the formal management of the payment system as practised in this firm was primarily seen as enforcing or reaffirming methods of payment in order to control 'slack values' and protect the grade structure — as laid down and agreed with the union. The requirements of local management and supervision, the labour markets, product markets and technology were regarded as an interference with the preferred method of payment. These situational factors were not related in the minds of many senior managers with the appropriateness of the method of payments used. The 'misfit' nature of the payment methods appeared to be a frequent source of dispute by putting the achievement of management objectives into direct conflict with operative objectives, and also affected the firm's relations with their customers on quality and delivery.

## (E) Bargaining Power Ltd.

### Escalating earnings, overmanning — union power?

This firm was a major production unit of a complex engineering group. As part of a policy of rationalisation, management were examining labour costs and production difficulties in the belief that disputes or output losses would probably have a more immediate and wider effect on unit costs in the rationalised group. Though most of their labour force were 'indirects' (paid on time-rates) it appeared that their 'direct' production workers (paid on piece-rates) were the major problem. Their piece-work scheme was subject to a high rate of 'wage drift' which in the past had increased the differential between the 'directs'' and 'indirects'' rates of earnings and had frequently led to increased earnings. This movement in earnings (which was not matched by increases in output) not only initiated movement in the firm's wage structure but, through subsequent inter-firm 'parity disputes', also contributed to the movement of wage structures of several other firms. Certain areas of the firm had been identified as being critical in the initiation of these 'wage drift' movements —

1. Press Shop
2. Assembly Shop
3. Paint Shop

In these particular areas the rise in the firm's labour costs was considered to be out of the control of management and they sought an improvement or change in payment methods that would achieve the following objectives:

(a) limit this wage drift
(b) consequently decrease the 'out-of-line' pressure between 'directs' and 'indirects'
(c) gain greater managerial influence over the payment system.

They considered the alternatives of:

(a) 'revitalising' their current payment system, i.e. re-establishing the effort-reward relation in the design of their piecework scheme;
(b) 'engineering out' those jobs causing drift, i.e. examining the possibility of redesigning those jobs or related aspects of those jobs in order to restrict or remove those factors (dimensions) that were contributing to earnings drift; or
(c) 'replacing' the scheme entirely, i.e. changing the basic design of their method of payment.

Management considered that it was possible to revitalise the current scheme with the unions' involvement or pursue 'engineering out' parts of the job structure without involving the unions. However they concluded that a revitalised or adjusted piecework system would still be inappropriate and the commitment of time and resources to either would be so great that they might as well change radically to the current best system of payment for their situation — which they identified as measured day work.

A profile analysis was completed of each of the three problem areas of the production complex. As their traditional basis for completing a scheme was 'the shop', each profile was completed on that basis.

The following profile scores were obtained for each area:-

|  | Effort | Accountability | RI | RD | NR |
|---|---|---|---|---|---|
| Assembly Shop | Energy | Group | 35 | 5 | 12 (24) |
| Paint Shop | Energy | Group | 32 | 6 | 12 (24) |
| Press Shop | Energy | Group | 32 | 10 | 12 (24) |

In each of these areas rates were fixed by the rate-setter who would bargain with the various groups of men for a price per unit. In this piecemeal manner the relationship between effort and reward was established in this situation. The rate-setters in the past had never bothered to examine methods, tools or equipment necessary for the operation.

Such considerations might have then weakened the piece-work scheme as might the practice of operatives to fail to agree the piece-rate with the rate-setter and then work at a slow rate in order to receive the fall-back time-rate. This time-rate was then used as a basis for bargaining up the piece-rate.

Resulting from the weaknesses of their payment systems they had now become the market leaders in payment, not only in their locality but for their industry. In this situation they had attempted to maintain output and control earning levels by not giving in on further pay increases but by increasing manning, i.e. reducing 'effort' instead of increasing the level of earnings ('reward'). Such increases in manning in some of the large groups made it possible to re-balance work within the group 'informally' when group size increased. But management's attempts to reduce the level of manning were restricted by a management and union agreement that the 'taking out of jobs' would not involve 'line re-balancing': it was almost impossible to take 'jobs out' of their production lines without having to re-balance it. An improvement or change in payment method might also resolve the built-in overmanning problem that had arisen from the management of their method of payment. Management hoped to introduce conversion rates that would relate work estimates to manning levels as well as levels of payment.

An examination of the profile patterns and scores for each of the three areas suggests that relatively few of the dimensions are 'misfits' to their current method of payment. The union had recently claimed that 'waiting time' be paid at the normal piece-rate rather than the lower day-rate, which seems to relate to the 'misfit' profile dimension (5) and (6), on all of the profiles — especially in the assembly shop. Unlike several firms, but as in firm D, operatives were not paid average when there was a dispute about pay — work stopped and as the workflow was highly integrated and there was little stock, the effect of a stoppage was significant.

The highest earnings were in fact obtained in the assembly area and consequently it had been more overmanned in an attempt to control the *level* of earnings. In the paint shop a high level of earnings was supplemented with many allowances that were give in this situation, though it was not mentioned what the allowances were given for; one prediction would be that they were associated with the high rate of product change in that shop. The press shop had the lowest level of earnings of the three, though their rate of product change was again high as they produced items for many of the other factories of the firm's group. The press shop, in particular, was said to benefit from 'differential issues' and had much smaller group schemes than those of either the assembly or paint shop. Apart from the 'misfit' dimensions already mentioned and the complex occupational structure, the other dimensions were not specifically commented on. However, the profiles need to be supplemented by the observations of the areas and the particular comments made by management on some of the profile dimensions.

Observation of the areas suggests that some of the dimensions scored by members of the firm did not fully represent the variation that existed, either within the area or possibly within the different work groups. For example, observation of the assembly shop suggests that the profiled situation was more complex than that scored on the dimensions. There was, for example, a wide range of different degrees of automation in this area. Hence, although the schemes were 'energy group' schemes, if the profile had taken account of the full range of machinery this complexity would have had implications for the appropriateness of one scheme for the whole area. This unrecorded variation in the area would have influenced dimensions (2), (4), (5), (6) and possibly (7). The degree of automation in particular requires the additional scoring of SPO in the assembly shop and paint shop, and CTM in the press shop. A more detailed analysis of the adminstrative basis of the group schemes via profile analysis might have suggested that they would have been better adminstratively based on, for example, 'machine groups' rather than the whole 'shop'.

The time period on which the profiles were completed did not take account of the periodic problems that occurred on the rate of product change dimension. Though the rate of product change was recorded as low in some areas, for

| 1(g) | Type of effort | Time | | | Energy | | | Competence | | | |
|---|---|---|---|---|---|---|---|---|---|---|---|
| 2(g) | Unit of accountability | Individual | | | Group | | | Plant | | | |
| | | 1 | 2 | 3 | 4 | 5 | 6 | 7 | 8 | 9 | |
| 1 | Length of job cycle | to 5 | 6-10 | 11-15 | 16-30 | 31-45 | 46-60 | 61-90 | 91-120 | 121+ | Mins. |
| 2. | Number of job modifications | 0 | 1 | 2 | 3 | 4 | 5 | 6 | 7 | 8+ | Av. no. per month |
| 3 | Degree of automation | SPT | PAT | SMT | CMT | STM | CTM | SPO | CPO | CCP | |
| 4 | Number of product changes | 0 | 1 | 2 | 3 | 4 | 5 | 6 | 7 | 8+ | Av. no. per month |
| 5 | Number of job stoppages | 0 | 1 | 2 | 3 | 4 | 5 | 6 | 7 | 8+ | Av. no. per day |
| 6 | Duration of job stoppages | 0 | 1-5 | 6-10 | 11-20 | 21-30 | 31-40 | 41-50 | 51-60 | 61+ | Av. no. m per day |
| 7 | % job elements specified by management | 71+ | 61-70 | 51-60 | 41-50 | 31-40 | 21-30 | 11-20 | 1-10 | 0 | % |
| 8 | % material scrapped | 0 | 1-2 | 3-4 | 5-6 | 7-8 | 9-10 | 11-12 | 13-14 | 15+ | % |
| 9 | % products/components rejected | 0 | 1-2 | 3-4 | 5-6 | 7-8 | 9-10 | 11-12 | 13-14 | 15+ | % |
| 10 | Time required to fill vacancy | 1 | 2-4 | 5-7 | 8-10 | 11-13 | 14-16 | 17-19 | 20-22 | 23+ | Days |
| 11 | Labour stability | 81+ | 71-80 | 61-70 | 51-60 | 41-50 | 31-40 | 21-30 | 11-20 | 0-10 | % |
| 12 | Labour turnover | 0 / 0 | 6 / 12 | 12 / 24 | 18 / 36 | 24 / 48 | 30 / 60 | 36 / 72 | 42 / 84 | 48 / 96 | Men Women |
| 13 | Disputes about pay | 0-4 | 5-8 | 9-12 | 13-16 | 17-20 | 21-24 | 25-28 | 29-32 | 33+ | Av. no. per month |
| 14 | Man hours lost in pay disputes | 0-4 | 5-8 | 9-12 | 13-16 | 17-20 | 21-24 | 25-28 | 29-32 | 33+ | % per month |
| 15 | % earnings decided outside plant/company | 0-10 | 11-20 | 21-30 | 31-40 | 41-50 | 51-60 | 61-70 | 71-80 | 81+ | % |
| 16 | Number of trade unions | 0 | 1-3 | 4-6 | 7-9 | 10-12 | 13-15 | 16-18 | 19-21 | 22+ | All plant |
| 17 | Occupational structure | 0-3 | 4-6 | 7-9 | 10-12 | 13-15 | 16-18 | 19-21 | 22-24 | 25+ | All plant |
| 18 | Absence | 0 | 2-3 | 4-5 | 6-7 | 8-9 | 10-11 | 12-13 | 14-15 | 16+ | % normal h |
| 19 | Average age of working force | 15-29 | | | 30-44 | | | 45+ | | | Years |
| 20 | % labour cost in unit cost | 23+ | 21-23 | 18-20 | 15-17 | 12-14 | 10-12 | 7-9 | 4-6 | 1-3 | % |
| 21 | % males in working force | 0 | to 10 | 11-20 | 21-30 | 31-40 | 41-50 | 51-60 | 61-70 | 71+ | % All plant |

*Figure 23.  Assembly Shop*

90

| Type of effort | Time | | | Energy | | | Competence | | | |
|---|---|---|---|---|---|---|---|---|---|---|
| Unit of accountability | Individual | | | Group | | | Plant | | | |
| | 1 | 2 | 3 | 4 | 5 | 6 | 7 | 8 | 9 | |
| Length of job cycle | to 5 | 6-10 | 11-15 | 16-30 | 31-45 | 46-60 | 61-90 | 91-120 | 121+ | Mins. |
| Number of job modifications | 0 | 1 | 2 | 3 | 4 | 5 | 6 | 7 | 8+ | Av. no. per month |
| Degree of automation | SPT | PAT | SMT | CMT | STM | CTM | SPO | CPO | CCP | |
| Number of product changes | 0 | 1 | 2 | 3 | 4 | 5 | 6 | 7 | 8+ | Av. no. per month |
| Number of job stoppages | 0 | 1 | 2 | 3 | 4 | 5 | 6 | 7 | 8+ | Av. no. per day |
| Duration of job stoppages | 0 | 1-5 | 6-10 | 11-20 | 21-30 | 31-40 | 41-50 | 51-60 | 61+ | Av. no. mins. per day |
| % job elements specified by management | 71+ | 61-70 | 51-60 | 41-50 | 31-40 | 21-30 | 11-20 | 1-10 | 0 | % |
| % material scrapped | 0 | 1-2 | 3-4 | 5-6 | 7-8 | 9-10 | 11-12 | 13-14 | 15+ | % |
| % products/components rejected | 0 | 1-2 | 3-4 | 5-6 | 7-8 | 9-10 | 11-12 | 13-14 | 15+ | % |
| Time required to fill vacancy | 1 | 2-4 | 5-7 | 8-10 | 11-13 | 14-16 | 17-19 | 20-22 | 23+ | Days |
| Labour stability | 81+ | 71-80 | 61-70 | 51-60 | 41-50 | 31-40 | 21-30 | 11-20 | 0-10 | % |
| Labour turnover | 0 / 0 | 6 / 12 | 12 / 24 | 18 / 36 | 24 / 48 | 30 / 60 | 36 / 72 | 42 / 84 | 48 / 96 | Men % / Women % |
| Disputes about pay | 0-4 | 5-8 | 9-12 | 13-16 | 17-20 | 21-24 | 25-28 | 29-32 | 33+ | Av. no. per month |
| Man hours lost in pay disputes | 0-4 | 5-8 | 9-12 | 13-16 | 17-20 | 21-24 | 25-28 | 29-32 | 33+ | % per month |
| % earnings decided outside plant/company | 0-10 | 11-20 | 21-30 | 31-40 | 41-50 | 51-60 | 61-70 | 71-80 | 81+ | % |
| Number of trade unions | 0 | 1-3 | 4-6 | 7-9 | 10-12 | 13-15 | 16-18 | 19-21 | 22+ | All plant |
| Occupational structure | 0-3 | 4-6 | 7-9 | 10-12 | 13-15 | 16-18 | 19-21 | 22-24 | 25+ | All plant |
| Absence | 0 | 2-3 | 4-5 | 6-7 | 8-9 | 10-11 | 12-13 | 14-15 | 16+ | % normal hours |
| Average age of working force | 15-29 | | | 30-44 | | | 45+ | | | Years |
| % labour cost in unit cost | 23+ | 21-23 | 18-20 | 15-17 | 12-14 | 10-12 | 7-9 | 4-6 | 1-3 | % |
| % males in working force | 0 | to 10 | 11-20 | 21-30 | 31-40 | 41-50 | 51-60 | 61-70 | 71+ | % All plant |

*Figure 24. Paint Shop*

| | | Time | | | Energy | | | Competence | | | |
|---|---|---|---|---|---|---|---|---|---|---|---|
| 1(g) | Type of effort | | | | | | | | | | |
| 2(g) | Unit of accountability | Individual | | | Group | | | Plant | | | |
| | | 1 | 2 | 3 | 4 | 5 | 6 | 7 | 8 | 9 | |
| 1 | Length of job cycle | to 5 | 6-10 | 11-15 | 16-30 | 31-45 | 46-60 | 61-90 | 91-120 | 121+ | Mins. |
| 2 | Number of job modifications | 0 | 1 | 2 | 3 | 4 | 5 | 6 | 7 | 8+ | Av. no. per month |
| 3 | Degree of automation | SPT | PAT | SMT | CMT | STM | CTM | SPO | CPO | CCP | |
| 4 | Number of product changes | 0 | 1 | 2 | 3 | 4 | 5 | 6 | 7 | 8+ | Av. no. per month |
| 5 | Number of job stoppages | 0 | 1 | 2 | 3 | 4 | 5 | 6 | 7 | 8 | Av. no. per day |
| 6 | Duration of job stoppages | 0 | 1-5 | 6-10 | 11-20 | 21-30 | 31-40 | 41-50 | 51-60 | 61+ | Av. no. m per day |
| 7 | % job elements specified by management | 71+ | 61-70 | 51-60 | 41-50 | 31-40 | 21-30 | 11-20 | 1-10 | 0 | % |
| 8 | % material scrapped | 0 | 1-2 | 3-4 | 5-6 | 7-8 | 9-10 | 11-12 | 13-14 | 15+ | % |
| 9 | % products/components rejected | 0 | 1-2 | 3-4 | 5-6 | 7-8 | 9-10 | 11-12 | 13-14 | 15+ | % |
| 10 | Time required to fill vacancy | 1 | 2-4 | 5-7 | 8-10 | 11-13 | 14-16 | 17-19 | 20-22 | 23+ | Days |
| 11 | Labour stability | 81+ | 71-80 | 61-70 | 51-60 | 41-50 | 31-40 | 21-30 | 11-20 | 0-10 | % |
| 12 | Labour turnover | | 6 12 | 12 24 | 18 36 | 24 48 | 30 60 | 36 72 | 42 84 | 48 96 | Men Women |
| 13 | Disputes about pay | 0-4 | 5-8 | 9-12 | 13-16 | 17-20 | 21-24 | 25-28 | 29-32 | 33+ | Av. no. per month |
| 14 | Man hours lost in pay disputes | 0-4 | 5-8 | 9-12 | 13-16 | 17-20 | 21-24 | 25-28 | 29-32 | 33+ | % per month |
| 15 | % earnings decided outside plant/company | 0-10 | 11-20 | 21-30 | 31-40 | 41-50 | 51-60 | 61-70 | 71-80 | 81+ | % |
| 16 | Number of trade unions | 0 | 1-3 | 4-6 | 7-9 | 10-12 | 13-15 | 16-18 | 19-21 | 22+ | All plant |
| 17 | Occupational structure | 0-3 | 4-6 | 7-9 | 10-12 | 13-15 | 16-18 | 19-21 | 22-24 | 25+ | All plant |
| 18 | Absence | 0 | 2-3 | 4-5 | 6-7 | 8-9 | 10-11 | 12-13 | 14-15 | 16+ | % normal H |
| 19 | Average age of working force | 15-29 | | | 30-44 | | | 45+ | | | Years |
| 20 | % labour cost in unit cost | 23+ | 21-23 | 18-20 | 15-17 | 12-14 | 10-12 | 7-9 | 4-6 | 1-3 | % |
| 21 | % males in working force | 0 | to 10 | 11-20 | 21-30 | 31-40 | 41-50 | 51-60 | 61-70 | 71+ | % All plan |

*Figure 25. Press Shop*

92

example, the assembly shop, this score was based on a completely new product design and did not account for the significant changes in production volume that occurred. These volume fluctuations on inflexible product lines with low stock levels, with no opportunity for labour redeployment, had an immediate impact on the 'standards' established for payment and manning. It was not then surprising that the initial setting of 'standards' of output for new products was considered important, with use being made of 'learning curves' to predict output. Management commented that the piecework scheme was usually satisfactory once piece-rates were fixed and the product sold well — however, if it did not sell well there tended to be pay disputes. Eventually, low volumes resulted in the men working a short week and they might then enter a labour pool before a redundancy policy was implemented. Such product cycle characteristics as well as the incidence of innovation in product design, coupled with fluctuating manpower requirements, would have an impact on the effectiveness of any scheme at these times. Such changes occurred over years rather than in the six month profiled period.

In addition to the analysis of the payment system provided by the Lupton-Gowler method, this firm had also evaluated the appropriateness of their pay scheme in a slightly different way. This is now detailed so it can be compared with the Lupton-Gowler method. The evaluation of the method of payment was undertaken by a small project group which spent several months analysing and examining their own and alternative methods of payment — discussing the appropriate levels of guarantees, assessing the effect of disputes and shortages within and outside the firm on differing methods of payment. An analysis of the effect of reaching various levels of output under their current piece-work scheme demonstrated that at the higher levels of output (which they planned to achieve) there was a change in the effort-reward relationship to the advantage of the men. They also analysed the spread of earnings (and the component parts of earnings) and plotted these against the grade structure for each site and analysed the impact that the different methods of payment had had on the levels of earnings achieved. This provided them with some managerial measure of control of the reward structure (though not 'effort' contributions). The different patterns of earnings at their different sites were mainly attributed to strong union differentials. The Lupton-Gowler method suggests that difficulties in maintaining and establishing the effort-reward relationship in their situation might be related to other factors than solely union power.

The project group then systematically assessed the requirements and expectations of the men, supervision and management on payment — in the latter two cases it was a matter of education in the alternatives and implication for the payment systems design and control. They held discussions with supervisors to establish:

1. The men's expected levels of pay
2. What the men expected of management in the near future
3. What method of payment the men preferred
4. The men's evaluation of the current fringe benefits
5. What the men thought of the review system of the current method of wage payment and the frequency of this review.

As part of the programme of changing the payment system, the project group completed a number of presentations to senior management to build up their confidence in changing the payment method — presentations were also to be given at a later stage to other management groups and eventually to the operatives. The project groups suggested to management that they could achieve the following with a change in payment methods: remove shop floor bargaining, rid themselves of differential issues, improve labour mobility, reduce 'levering' to bargain rates with new methods, reduce the influence of the shop steward, relate payment to the size of the labour force, standardise performance and improve the acceptance of planning. However, they did not mention whether these objectives conflicted, but presumably considered that measured day work would give them all these advantages. This list might be presumed to reflect some of the problems raised with their current payment system in their situation. They realised that a change to measured day work would be related to making management more experienced in handling 'standards' of the 'effort' component, as the 'reward' component would now be fixed. To assist in improving this monitoring, they also planned to change from bargained rate-fixing to time-study methods of establishing performance standards and appreciated that the new methods of payment would have implications for quality control, some administrative systems, education, training, engineering, planning and the industrial relations department. As the new payment scheme would also be characterised by different 'bargaining issues' (see firms B and C) they had prepared negotiation briefs to show the consequences of the alternative types of action that might be taken with the new payment method.

The project group's and management's expectations were that the new payment scheme in their particular situation would achieve their current objectives and provide additional longer term benefits from productivity improvement within the firm, i.e.

1. Bring the 'direct' workers' payment into line with that of the 'indirect' workers and to limit future 'wage drift.'
2. Create an atmosphere for proper work standards which would form the basis for future productivity and control. This was the first time that the company had used time study measurement.
3. Ensure that acceptable unit costs on expected performance standards were reached.
4. Be acceptable to the unions and the men concerned.

The method of payment would also be related to work schedules and 'recognised' manning levels.

## Conclusion for Bargaining Power Ltd.

The central position of the production unit in the group's production network, the highly integrated nature of the particular production process and the periodic product market fluctuations might have contributed to the apparent weaknesses in rate-fixing and supervision. Though the earnings differential disputes might be reduced if the grade structure were rationalised and the reward structure fixed, the circumstances still exist for 'effort' and 'effort differential' disputes. Under a measured day work method of payment management bears the cost of the utilisation of its labour force due to factors either within or outside its control, whereas under an incentive type of scheme the cost is directly borne by the labour force. However, as the new method of payment was to be accompanied by improvements in managerial controls (as far as this is possible) i.e. steadier schedule levels and less product change, the incident of 'effort' disputes might then be reduced though they would not be completely eliminated. One could argue that the effectiveness of the *current* scheme could have been improved by moving profile dimensions (4), (5) and (6) and rationalising the occupational structure (17), though such changes might have been impossible or very costly. Such 'misfit' dimensions would still weaken the new payment method.

Observation of the areas also suggested that the adminstrative basis of the schemes, i.e. the large group schemes, did not match the situational complexity of the areas e.g. the diverse technological mix, product mix and volume fluctuations. This administrative mismatch also contributed to the weakening of their payment system. Their proposed, more detailed, administration of the area under measured day work would probably improve the new payment 'fit' primarily by improving the adminstrative 'fit' to the situation.

Their method of selecting a wage payment system was much more detailed than that adopted in any of the previous firms. However, its focus on the level of earnings and on obtaining operator agreement with the method of payment, though important, overlooked many of the circumstances that might still weaken their new method of payment, i.e. the bargaining problems that might still arise from their product and market strategies, their plant design, their production technology, their low stock levels and the high dependence of the rest of the group's activities on this particular unit.

*Union power was more likely to be the result of this type of situation — not the cause.* The success of the new method of payment, i.e. with a fixed reward, would depend on how far supervision and management could now manage the 'effort' standards under the pressure of these 'misfit' dimensions. The structure and level of payment in the particular areas analysed were probably more influenced by the impact of some of the 'misfit' dimensions over periods of years rather than a six month period: the time period recommended by Lupton and Gowler. Though the main changes in the pay structure appear to have come through the movement of piece-rates, payment was also supplemented by 'non-performance allowances' (particularly in the paint shop) i.e. payments unrelated to output. The weaknesses described in the payment system suggests that in this situation it was difficult to relate effort and reward in the piece-work rules, and that as in firm D the 'energy' schemes may have in fact become 'time'. One manager's comment that at times 'the men played chess on the production lines', though initially considered by the writer as a joke, might well have indicated the condition of the firm's payment scheme and the firm's management of the payment situation. The rise in labour costs (via earnings movements and overmanning) and their proposed change in payment methods was not unrelated to past inappropriate payment system design. It appears that to succeed in meeting their objectives, substantial situational changes would be required in addition to the payment rule changes that they had already made.

# 4    Comments on the Practical Application

In this part comments are made on the formulation of the Lupton-Gowler procedure and the experience of its application.

The authors stated that their procedure for selecting a payment system needed to be tested out by experimentation and by the appraisal of the results of such experimentation, so that its feasibility could be realistically assessed. Unfortunately, the approach they adopted to diagnose and select payment systems was so novel that many managers had difficulty in recounciling it with accepted and conventional practices of selecting and diagnosing payment systems. This led some to reject it rather than experiment and test out the ideas underlying the procedure.

So that the reader can refer back to the corresponding sections of the original Lupton-Gowler text the comments are ordered under the following main headings:

The Logical Classification of Payment Systems
The Profile Dimensions — Definition and Measurement
The Procedure for Matching Situation and Payment
Assumptions, Values and Objectives of Payment

## The Logical Classification of Payment Systems

Lupton and Gowler make two major claims:

- all payment schemes are in essence similar
- the logical classification of payment systems corresponds with all known payment systems.

Though payment schemes are similar in terms of the logic of attempting to relate 'reward' and 'effort', there appear to be significant differences between 'energy' as opposed to the 'time' and 'competence' schemes and perhaps greater practical similarities between the reciprocal deferred and non-reciprocal types of schemes. The main differences between 'energy' (output related) schemes and 'time' and 'competence' schemes is that under such energy schemes 'effort' and 'reward' are required to be made explicit, as are the rules for relating 'effort' and 'reward' e.g. in piecework, incentive bonus and some forms of measured-day-work; whereas under 'time' and 'competence' schemes the establishment and re-establishment of the 'effort' and 'reward' aspects of payment might be too complex to formalise into an explicit set of rules on payment or might not be considered to be worthwhile or possible. The 'time' basis for payment frequently just required attendance; and 'competence' may or may not require demonstrated performance. In both these cases supervision and management might make more use of social and psychological rewards to establish 'effort' (if required) and so in this respect 'time' and 'competence'[10] schemes are markedly different from 'energy' schemes, a distinction noted but not sufficiently emphasized by Lupton and Gowler (Figure 26). Supervision might then play an important part in relating reward and effort under a time scheme, or in the case of a competence scheme, a skilled employee might be given a great deal of discretion in his work contribution, supervision and management abdicating to this type of 'effort'. The application of profile analysis to situations being examined for or currently operating with 'energy' schemes proved to be particularly interesting, as the level and structure of the pay packet was directly related to some of the situation's dimensions.

[10] It was thought that the classification of 'work simplification' as CRD was to confuse payment with certain work study techniques that could be applied to any scheme. However, Lupton and Gowler commented that in this particular case they thought that work-study techniques were used as an aid to performance improvement. The assumption is that if the resulting improvement is rewarded, then people will be motivated to use the techniques and they suggested that a better description would be 'schemes based on work simplification techniques'.

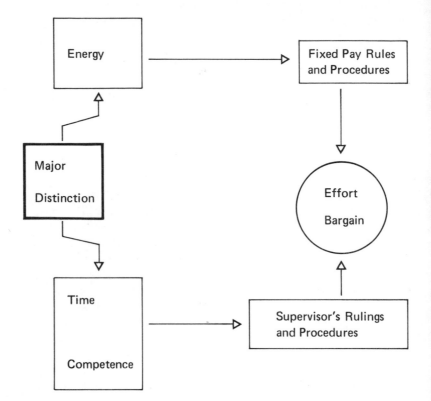

*Figure 26. Major Payment Systems*

The distinction made between reciprocal deferred and non-reciprocal schemes also seems to ignore the practical similarities between such schemes i.e. many deferred payments are fairly stable elements of the pay packet. This is due to the fact that they are often calculated over a long period of time and usually for large groups, if not for a whole firm — both of which must weaken the relation between 'reward' and 'effort'. Frequently the so-called deferred element of payment of productivity bonus comes to be regarded as a fairly stable part of the pay packet by both men and management — and so is similar in effect to a non-reciprocal element. ⌡

The Lupton-Gowler scheme assumes, as do many managers, that payment systems maintain their characteristics over long periods of time. In fact, some managers 'tinker' with schemes in order to solve short-term problems, or they allow workers to 'tinker' with them. The result may well be that the formal description of the scheme as it was first installed, and which is still used to describe it, is no longer appropriate. The 'tinkering' has pushed the system into another box in the grid. Altering the gearing of a system so as to equalise the bonus earnings of workers whose effort is similar, or placing a 'ceiling output', whether imposed by management or the work group, may transform what is apparently a reciprocal immediate scheme into a non-reciprocal one.

For example, typical, and in some firms prescribed, practice when an incentive bonus scheme 'fails' in a highly variable work situation is:

(a) to increase the 'bonus' element
(b) gear the scheme, and
(c) use a larger unit of accountability.

This logic conflicts with the Lupton-Gowler notion of consolidating rather than fragmenting a pay packet in highly variable situations[11] and it is suggested that each of the above modifications would make the reciprocal immediate scheme more similar in effect to a reciprocal deferred or non-reciprocal scheme and *not* improve a reciprocal immediate scheme effectiveness. 'Tinkering' usually reflects management's preoccupation with the 'reward' (and reward differentials) rather than the 'effort' aspect of the payment system. The result of such dysfunctional 'tinkering' though it may overcome some short-term problem primarily by

---

[11] If the reader looks back to the examples this tends to be confirmed i.e. successful 'energy' schemes are associated with the reciprocal immediate situation and pressures for consolidation come from the reciprocal deferred or non-reciprocal characteristics.

adjusting the payment rules, might result in such behaviour as restricting output, starting work late or finishing work early, overmanning, undermining supervisory authority and so on.

The logical classification scheme corresponded with all the payment systems examined in this survey, though during the survey managers often employed definitions of methods of payment that did not correspond to those in the Lupton-Gowler classification. Sometimes reference was made to other sets of definitions, in support of a manager's claim that his definition was right, or out of a reluctance to use the Lupton-Gowler classification and to see its implications for his own situation. In short, some managers had difficulty in harmonising their own way of describing and classifying payment systems, and 'he terminology employed by Lupton and Gowler. This is not surprising because the manager's classification will be descriptive and incomplete, whereas the Lupton-Gowler scheme aims to be analytical and exhaustive; but it indicates that a manager might find it difficult to abandon his own modes of classification and definition and accept and work with a more complex and abstract alternative. This might be taken to pose a problem of communication and training; however, from the previous examples and subject to the qualifications made in this section, the reader should have little difficulty in identifying the appropriate box for their current proposed scheme in the Lupton-Gowler classification.

Summary of points

1. There is a major distinction between 'energy' and 'time/competence' payment schemes.
2. In practice there appears to be a strong similarity between reciprocal deferred and non-reciprocal payment schemes.
3. The effect of 'tinkering' with payment schemes is often overlooked.
4. The logical classification scheme corresponded with the payment systems examined.

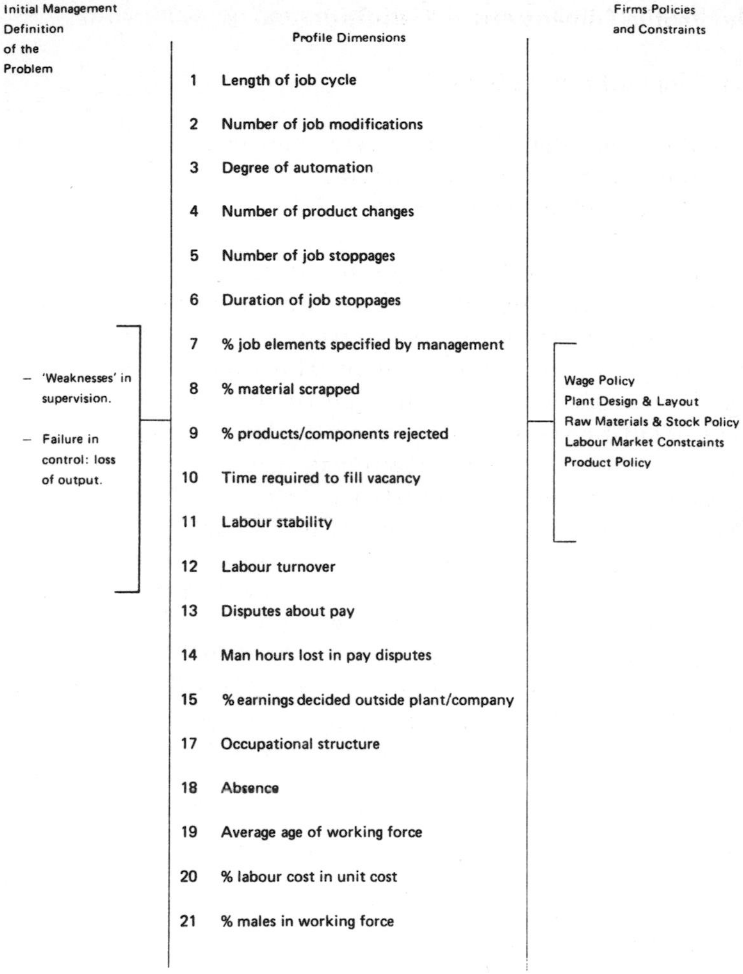

Initial Management
Definition
of the
Problem

Profile Dimensions

Firms Policies
and Constraints

1   Length of job cycle

2   Number of job modifications

3   Degree of automation

4   Number of product changes

5   Number of job stoppages

6   Duration of job stoppages

7   % job elements specified by management

− 'Weaknesses' in
  supervision.

8   % material scrapped

Wage Policy
Plant Design & Layout
Raw Materials & Stock Policy
Labour Market Constraints
Product Policy

− Failure in
  control: loss
  of output.

9   % products/components rejected

10  Time required to fill vacancy

11  Labour stability

12  Labour turnover

13  Disputes about pay

14  Man hours lost in pay disputes

15  % earnings decided outside plant/company

17  Occupational structure

18  Absence

19  Average age of working force

20  % labour cost in unit cost

21  % males in working force

*Figure 27. The Profile Dimensions and Policies and Constraints of Firm C*

103

## The Profile Dimensions — Definition and Measurement

Here the authors claimed that:

— they had identified the circumstances that influence the operation of payment systems.
— these circumstances could be defined and measured.

All of the profile dimensions were commented on by management and the rationale for their inclusion seems to be well substantiated by the description of their impact on the various types of payment systems. However, it was rarely the case in any particular firm that *all* of the profile dimensions were identified by management as being relevant to the operation of payment systems; certainly, some were considered of little importance e.g. 'age structure' or 'percentage of males in the labour force'. Similarly, it cannot be claimed that the profile scores always identified the circumstances in the same terms as management might have construed them. For example, in firm C although numerous 'misfits' were recorded it was not possible to relate this specifically to their particular policies and current constraints solely from the profile score, though it is apparent that many of the 'misfit' dimensions owed a great deal to such policies or environmental constraints (Figure 27).

The actual process of collecting the profile data therefore is useful in making an 'outsider' very quickly aware of other aspects of the payment system which, though not scored on the profile dimensions, would obviously have implications for the interpretation of the dimensions e.g. the adequacy of management information, the nature of the operational problems that produced certain dimensional patterns, the relatedness of certain dimensions and an appreciation of how far the 'average' score is representative or whether the time period on which the analysis is based is typical or atypical. The latter point was particularly important in firms where a dimension or set of dimensions would change radically over a period of time. This limitation, i.e. that profile analysis is usually based on six monthly averages, cannot be neatly resolved apart from drawing it to the reader's attention. The utility of the procedure is undoubtedly limited by the availability and quality of the profile information. The information required to complete the procedure of 'profiling' was frequently drawn from many sources.

Work study, production scheduling and quality control usually supplied the technical data. Information on the labour market, training periods, absence, disputes and the occupational structure was sought from personnel, costs from the accounts department and so on. However, in the absence of information on one or more of the dimensions, a qualified estimate might be used in the analysis. In the firms surveyed there were only a few instances when information did not exist to guide the scoring of the dimensions. The method of payment the firm currently employed might determine the availability or accuracy of the information obtained, e.g. detailed records might be kept on job stoppages under an incentive scheme but not under a payment by the hour scheme.

When selecting the area to be examined it might be found that areas presumed to be different are, in profile terms, similar and those that may have been treated as the same in the past might be different — hence it might be possible to identify the better administrative areas as the basis for schemes. The profile is most useful in pointing out similarities and differences that are usually missed by casual or blinkered observation. For example, a comparative profile analysis as undertaken in some firms of all the main areas of the firm was a useful application. Conducting the analysis in one area brought to light the cause of the problems in another area e.g. to retain labour in the machine shop in a tight labour market, supervision might have set a lower standard of precision in the machining of parts, to increase earnings under the shop incentive scheme, though this might then disrupt the effectiveness of the incentive scheme in the assembly shop of the firm, where they would have difficulty in fitting the badly machined parts. In this way the problem of maintaining the payment system in the machine shop is 'transmitted' to the assembly shop. Weaknesses in the payment system of maintainance and service groups often have similar impact on the 'directs' in the production areas of a firm. The interrelatedness of such groups or departments might then create particular problems in managing the differentials both of effort and reward in a firm.

The majority of profiles (as are the administrative areas of payment) are usually completed on the basis of 'the shop' or department. This approach is satisfactory if the profile pattern represents the characteristics of the situation and is stable over the time period considered for scoring. In some firms it was doubtful how far the given scheme could possibly be 'matched' to the complexity of some areas. One became aware of this as one completed the profile dimensions — as for example with dimensions (4), (5), and (6) of the Misto Plant.

It might be assumed that it is always best to base a scheme and hence the profile analysis at the level of the individual; and management preferences for 'individually' based schemes rather than aggregated group or plant schemes seemed to be based on the idea that 'individual' schemes are more effective. But in firm D the widespread application of 'individual' and 'small group' schemes disregarded the impact of the technology and the periodic requirement for re-deployment between groups and jobs. The requirements of the situation might have been better understood had the level of analysis taken account of 'plant and process' behaviour rather than solely focusing on individual behaviour in this particular case. Similarly, on integrated machining lines the application of individual schemes, which then, of course, reward individual performance, was incompatible with highly integrated and sequential product line development where variations in individual performance required and allowed by such a scheme could well disrupt production. Yet again, firms with a highly complex occupational structure might not consider individually based schemes best suited to their situation. If one expects that there might be a marked discrepancy on an individual, group or plant basis one might obtain additional information for the particular dimensions concerned. A decision on the unit of accountability has important implications for the consequent administration of the scheme, production scheduling and the bargaining structure that is then created. For if one pays on an

106

individual, group or plant basis, this divisive or integrating aspect will reinforce or further divide the total characteristics of the area. As this might hinder production this aspect of payment design should not be overlooked. Of course major situational changes in an area might require the re-evaluation of the administrative basis of the payment methods in that area. This observation which followed from the completion of the profile and consideration of the alternatives under the headings of accountability, was frequently overlooked — situational changes rarely prompted a reconsideration of the basis of the scheme, with, for example, a reorganisation of the basis of the scheme, or a major production reorganisation from process production to product line production. Though the Lupton-Gowler method does not give sufficient guidance on the implications of selecting the unit of accountability the above comments should improve this. No hard and fast rules appear to exist for deciding the area of unit of accountability. An evaluation of the effect of changing accountability on the various profile dimensions might be the most effective form of assessment.

Having decided the appropriate area or unit of production the next decision is to score the type of 'effort'. The method itself provides no measure of 'effort' or 'reward' but it does have implications for the rules and procedures that might be adopted to relate 'effort' and 'reward'. As was mentioned previously, there appears to be a greater difference between 'energy' type of schemes and 'time' and 'competence' types of schemes. In terms of the profile dimensions both payment by the hour and payment for competence usually meant that many of the profile dimensions varied considerably. An examination of dimensions (1) and (7) might be important if an 'energy' scheme was considered, i.e. it might be found that increased specification might be difficult or uneconomic. The re-categorisation of the types of effort may be necessary if certain improvements or changes are made to the firm's situation, e.g. increasing mechanisation might require a move to 'competence' schemes or a change in product policy might require large volumes of standard products which might be better suited to an 'energy' type of scheme. Further comments on the profile dimensions that might assist in the interpretation and technical application of the profile appear in Chapter Five. Though the authors would not claim the operational definitions or measures to be flawless, they do appear to have some general utility in identifying the circumstances that influence the operation of payment systems. In all of the examples the profile added more relevant information to the managers' knowledge of the situation than they initially possessed, and focused their attention on, for example, how absenteeism affected the working of the payment system rather than considering that absence with a medical certificate was 'acceptable'. The authors simply asked managers to examine their firm by completing the profile dimensions so that management can clearly see the characteristics of their current payment system before considering changing it and systematically examine the implications of change in terms of operator, supervisor, or managerial 'efforts'.

### Summary of points

1. Management's evaluation of the significance of 'misfits' varied considerably although the rationale for the inclusion of all of the dimensions was supported.
2. Any radical changes on the profile dimensions beyond the six month period on which they are scored needs to be noted.
3. There is no clear guidance on deciding the area of unit of accountability on which the profile is completed.
4. The definitions and measures appear to have some general utility.

## The Procedure for Matching Situation and Payment

The authors claim it is possible to match situation with payment method. There are two main aspects of 'fit' in the matching of situation and payment method:

(a) the *logical 'fit'* between the profile measures and the attributed R.I. R.D. and N.R. scores.

(b) the *actual 'fit'* between the actual profile pattern and the implications for situational or payment method change in a particular context.

Originally, the 'Master Block' scores matched the logical classification of payment systems to the situational dimensions and suggested that the main methods of payment were *only* appropriate to certain situations, i.e. they were distinct and exclusive. However, in practice it appears that the *logical fit* for ANY payment method is the reciprocal immediate type of profile situation. The diagram of the revised logic of alternatives (Figure 28) then includes reciprocal deferred and non-reciprocal schemes as alternatives to the reciprocal immediate scheme (in the 'ideal' RI situation). The existence of reciprocal deferred and non-reciprocal scores should then be considered to be disruptive to the effort-reward relationship of all types of payment schemes. In terms of the original Lupton-Gowler logic reciprocal deferred and non-reciprocal scores would indicate that it would be just as difficult to relate 'effort' and 'reward' under an incentive method of payment as it would be to relate 'effort' and 'reward' under a consolidated method of payment. Though for reasons explained previously the relation between 'effort' and 'reward' is maintained differently in 'energy' as opposed to 'time/competence' schemes[12], as management and operatives' relations and their sensitivity to the 'effort bargain' usually differs with the different schemes.

In terms of the *actual fit* between payment method and the situation examined the authors are simply asking what the implications are for the effectiveness of the payment system if the 'misfit' dimensions are managed under the different main types of payment rules they had identified, and suggesting the possibilities of restructuring the pay packet or restructuring the situation to improve payment system 'fit'.

[12] Most of these differences are explored in an article by T. Lupton entitled *Methods of Wage Payment, Organisational Change and Motivation* in *Work Study and Management,* December 1964 where he outlines *in general* the organizational requirements necessary for piecework and controlled daywork schemes.

Original logic of alternatives represented on the profile:

| R.I. | R.D. | N.R. |
|------|------|------|

Revised logic of alternatives:

| R.I. | Examine 'Misfit' implications |
|------|------|
| R.D. | of |
| N.R. | Profile Dimensions. |

*Figure 28. Alternative Methods of Payment*

The main emphasis in the examples of the application of the procedure tended to stress the possibility of situational improvement rather than a detailed discussion of the pay packet structures. Lupton and Gowler did however suggest that the actual mixture of R.I., R.D. and N.R. scores might form the basis of the pay packet structure. This specific approach does not appear to be very satisfactory though there does appear to be some scope for including particular elements of payment that match certain situational characteristics.

To some extent the different basic payment rules design did facilitate or limit the types of adjustments that were made to the pay packet — for example one can compare the changes in firm C (the growth of overtime, grade and

110

allowance payments) with those in firm E (growth of piecework payment). Under an incentive scheme the deterioration in the effort-reward relationship often led to the type of 'erosion' that might 'penalise' or 'over reward' operatives unrelated to their effort; whereas under consolidated schemes the 'erosion' or failure of the payment system to relate 'reward' and 'effort' often resulted in a loss of effort (output). As the profile analysis seemed to be particularly useful in assessing the implications of applying 'energy' schemes to certain situations, the assumptions of such schemes will be examined first and then compared with 'time' and 'competence' schemes.

In the design of 'energy' schemes assumptions about the characteristic of the situation are built into the 'standards' or 'work values' which are then used as the basis for relating 'effort' and 'reward'. These assessments often ignore the 'misfit' implications of many of the dimensions of the situation (that operative 'efforts' might only be capable of influencing a few dimensions) and assume a degree of stability of the 'fit' and 'misfit' characteristics of the situation to which they are applied. In the latter case 'allowances' might be formally recognised in the pay packet to compensate for the impact of 'misfit' dimensions on the effort-reward relationship. All such assumptions about the characteristics and stability of the situation are translated into fixed payment rules. A change in the situation either by the development of additional 'misfit' dimensions or via the variability of one or more 'misfit' dimensions will undermine the assumptions on which the design of the payment scheme is based. In such situations the inappropriate design of the payment rules often leads to the payment system developing an 'independent existence'; and as under such schemes operatives directly bear the costs (or benefits) of their inappropriateness in their pay packet, this would heighten the sensitivity of such schemes to disputes or lead operatives to develop strategies to maintain stable and equitable efforts and earnings. Such attempts to stabilise the effort-reward relationship might lead to the creation of 'loose' bonus schemes, the further payment of 'allowances' or other ways of making up pay.

111

Although the reciprocal payment rules provided the main link between 'effort' and 'reward' in the various forms of 'energy' schemes, in the case of 'time' and 'competence' schemes this relationship is usually maintained differently. Payment is given for attendance rather than actual achievement, and cooperation with supervision and management is assessed and rewarded rather than a carefully measured contribution to the firm's output. Supervisory rulings and pressures (social and psychological rewards) link 'effort' and 'reward' under these schemes — where this is possible. Such schemes would have been a better 'fit' in those situations where the assumptions of the 'energy' payment rules did not match the realities of the situation. The consolidated basis of these schemes means that supervisory shortcomings in managing the 'effort' and 'reward' relationship are at a cost to management rather than the operative. The effectiveness of these types of schemes is dependent on the quality and pressures on supervision in their particular work situation. Supervisors' assumptions about the situation and the place of operative 'effort' in such situations may or may not be more realistic than the impersonal rules of 'energy' schemes. However, management sensitivity to these types of situations often needs to be greater that it would be if 'energy' schemes were used (where operative sensitivity to the situation is probably greater). Compare firms B and D.

In practice, when 'misfit' dimensions occurred the most usual forms of adjustment to the pay packet included giving allowances, booking 'extra' allowances, giving overtime and making up pay. Claims might be made for additional payments above the consolidated rates just as claims might be made for increased payment under incentive schemes when the effort-reward relationship is disturbed. The pay packet might then be restructured by 'misfit' dimensions not accounted for in the basic pay packet design which may require additional or substitute payments to be made. When this occurs such elements usually become part of an operative's wage expectation even though the circumstances that gave rise to its inclusion may have been remedied. The current structure of many pay packets often includes some 'historical' payments.

The payments that were observed to be associated with one or more 'misfit' dimensions are given in the following classification though in most cases there is rarely a one to one relationship between a 'misfit' dimension and an element of payment (which represents an additional or compensatory payment to stabilise the effort-reward relationship). *The rationale for including or excluding a payment element should be carefully examined in the light of the current situation and future changes.* This table cannot claim to be exhaustive — other 'allowances' or 'elements' exist though these payments should help the reader to consider some of the possible elements that might be included in the pay packet. A decision to include such elements should be undertaken in the knowledge of the 'dimensions' of the current situation and their stability in the future.

| Elements of Payment | Misfit Dimensions |
|---|---|
| Training Allowance | (3) (4) (10) (11) (12) |
| Skill & Flexibility Allowance | (1) (3) (4) (7) |
| Age Allowance (seniority, length of service) | (11) (12) (19) (21) |
| Material Allowances | (8) (9) (22) |
| Merit Award | (1) (7) |
| Responsibility Allowance | (1) (2) |
| Start-up, Development Allowance | (3) (4) |
| Stoppages Allowance | (5) (6) |
| Dispute Payment | (13) (14) |
| Change-over Allowance | (4) |

However, the existence of these additional or substitute elements of payment does not exclude the possibility that 'misfits' might also be compensated by variations in the size of the main elements of the pay packet i.e. bonus, piecework or time elements. Similarly, overtime payment might be an additional payment to cope with technological or labour market difficulties just as it might also be a functional 'differential' if the firm has a complex occupational structure. The actual size of the elements in the pay packet might vary considerably as might the different relationships between the payment elements. The types of elements that might be included will vary with the types of effort and an individual pay packet might also include additions influenced by other working groups. The Lupton-Gowler method then opens up a completely new perspective on payment system design and the possibility in some instances of 'optional' payment design. A review of the structure of the pay packet might take into account whether it might develop 'generally' (with few elements) or 'particularly' (with many elements) with the clear recognition of these additional payments and how such pay packets 'fit' the different situational characteristics of the firm.

'Misfit' characteristics also led to the restructuring of the situation by operatives, supervision and management in attempting to stabilise the effort-reward relationship. Supervisors helped out by doing operative work themselves, redefined work, overmanned and 'obscured' standards. Similarly operatives, supervision, and management attempted to maintain the effort-reward relationship by developing certain 'working practices'. Though these were frequently described as 'bad or restrictive practices' in many instances these adjustments to the pay packet or the situation represented the only types of adjustments they could make within the contraints of their influence over the particular situation. However, in most cases it appeared that there was potential for situational restructuring that would have made a substantial improvement to the payment system and might have eliminated the need for such practices. Figure 29 outlines the importance of the profile dimensions in deciding between the alternatives of restructuring the situation or re-structuring the pay packet.

However, there were cases where the most flexible aspect of the situation was the supervisory role. A change in supervisory skills or objectives might have an important impact on the situation. Where, for example, a payment scheme exists in a production situation that requires careful allocation of work between supervisor and operator — a new supervisor who is ignorant of the skill within a group might, via bad work allocation, disrupt the scheme. The supervisor's role in work scheduling, inspection, dealing with technical

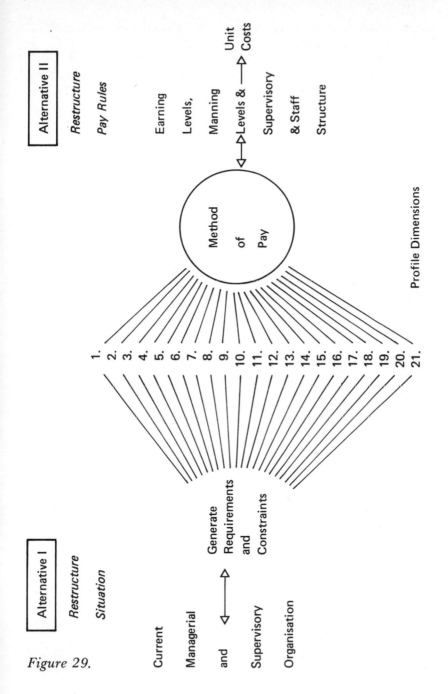

*Figure 29.*

Alternative II

*Restructure*

*Pay Rules*

Earning
Levels,
Manning
Levels &
Supervisory
& Staff
Structure

Unit
Costs

Method
of
Pay

Profile Dimensions

1.
2.
3.
4.
5.
6.
7.
8.
9.
10.
11.
12.
13.
14.
15.
16.
17.
18.
19.
20.
21.

Generate
Requirements
and
Constraints

Alternative I

*Restructure*

*Situation*

Current
Managerial
and
Supervisory
Organisation

problems and training all contribute to the management of the payment system.

Supervisors' assessment of performance might be formally included by involving them in decisions on payment through grade or merit awards, or this might be achieved inadvertently in the 'make-up' of payment under an inappropriate payment method, or by relating both supervisory and operative 'efforts', for example, by tying in a supervisory bonus with the work group they are supervising. In some instances where they have control over the flow of work they can then use this to reward appropriate behaviour. As part of the design of the payment system a thorough examination of the requirements of the supervisory role might be necessary to assess if the supervisor's skills match the situation and anticipated changes in the situation — for example, certain dimensions might indicate the need for skill in coping with high rates of product innovation, operative training or dealing with technological process problems. Improvements or changes in supervisory behaviour might have a substantial impact on the profiled situation. Although reference has been made to the assumptions about the improvement of situational 'fit' and the stability of the situation in the design of 'energy' schemes, supervision and management that is itself inflexible and insensitive to the effects of the 'misfit' dimensions on operative efforts might be as disruptive as 'energy' schemes *if* the situation required flexibility. 'Misfit' dimensions might reflect weaknesses in supervisory and managerial organisation as well as in the payment system.

One example of the frequent failure to 'fit' payment methods and situational characteristics often occurs in productivity bargaining. Some firms attempt to improve their situation by dealing solely with the payment rules — 'buying out' allowances, overtime, breaks, consolidating payment, all of which may not change the situational requirements that may have given rise to such pay rules e.g. buying out 'breaks' would not increase output if operatives are primarily constrained by limited machine capacity and material shortages. Such adjustments would only result in increased labour costs per unit. Similarly, the consolidation of the pay packet without improved supervisory and management organisation might lead to a rapid deterioration in output. An examination of changes in the situational dimensions in different parts of a firm might explain how certain elements associated with payment such as overtime, allowances, etc. which management thought it had 'bought out' had crept back into the pay packet. Certainly, many managers recognised that some misfit characteristics had in their experience a more concrete and immediate impact on the payment system than others e.g. a claim for 'allowances' for stoppages by 'direct' operatives, whereas the development of other dimensional misfits might grow gradually and less dramatically, e.g. absence might increase with an ageing labour force, or in terms of payment, increasing levels of overtime might be paid to a firm's maintenance groups to cope with the increasing erratic incidence of breakdowns of aged and overloaded plant.

By attempting to match situation and payment method this revealed the mistaken assumptions of some managements about their payment system i.e. that they were in complete control of the situations they were managing. The characteristics of their technology, plant design, product market and labour market might be such that they are in fact unable to control many of the factors that influence their payment system. Management themselves are in fact unable to guarantee equity of earnings and efforts in such situations though they might presume to do so by new methods and agreements on payment. *In such 'impossible' situations it would be mistaken to believe that control over the payment system is necessarily regained by sharing it with the unions involved — both might be victims of circumstances beyond their control.* Consequently, administrative attempts to formulate a coherent and rational industrial relations policy via an 'orderly' pay structure, and agreed rules and procedures, might be short-lived if the situations within the firm are not similarly coherent or rational (i.e. profile areas differ radically and are characterised by numerous 'misfit' dimensions).

The procedure for matching situation and payment method is a very useful exercise for managers to undertake.

117

The relatively clear cut strategies of

1. Changing the 'misfit' dimensions on the profile in line with the requirements of the type of payment system, or
2. Changing the method of payment to 'fit' with the current situational configuration,

should be reviewed in the light of an examination of what the actual 'misfit' consequences are, and if 'misfits' cannot be changed how far can improved supervision and management minimise their impact on the payment system. Much of this is best resolved in the final evaluation procedure, though systematic profile analysis within the firms might reveal the detailed attempts that have already been made to stabilise the 'effort' and 'reward' relationships (Figure 30) in the current situation.

often-overlooked 'eroding' factors of a payment system. The illusion of success with a change in payment methods is too often attributed to the nature of the payment rules themselves, and too little attention is paid to the situational improvements that accompany such change and the effect on the profile dimensions of the increased payment that accompanies such changes. By drawing attention to the 'misfit' dimensions Lupton and Gowler are asking managers to examine how far, for example, the rate of product change 'erodes' the payment method, or how effective is the consolidated grade structure in protecting the firm from labour market pressures, parity disputes and disruptions to the flow of work. On the whole it appears that the revised procedure of matching payment method and situation is more simple than the authors originally stated. Undoubtedly the 'misfit' profile dimensions indicate the factors that management should consider to assess how well they are managing their payment system. The matching procedure puts the payment system as the means of relating operator effort and reward in context and also indicates the productive potential that might come from improved supervisory and managerial organisation, which in itself may not require changes in payment methods or the pay packet structure. Following profile analysis, it should be possible to clarify the structure of 'authorities and responsibilities' between shop floor management and senior management as the basis for a firm's industrial relations policy. Certain firms might also appreciate that misfit dimensions might be better managed if certain managerial skills, techniques or policies were 'matched' with the misfit dimensions; for example, the use of learning curves adopted to cope with certain rate of product change characteristics (dimension 4), changes made to training policies (dimension 10) and so on.

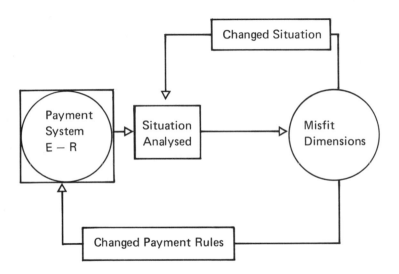

*Figure 30. Stabilising the Effort-Reward Relationship of the Payment System*

Summary of points
1. The 'ideal' logical situation for ANY payment system is the R.I. situation and one should expect that as one moves away or towards the R.I. situation changes take place in the effort-reward relationship.
2. All types of payment systems should be examined to

assess what impact a change in the payment rules in themselves would have on the dimensions of the situation examined.

3. The procedure has drawn attention to the fact that the logic of the pay rules are themselves rarely at fault but weaknesses in payment systems are often the result of the interaction of the pay rules in the situation to which they are applied. Consequently situational changes (sometimes with payment rule changes) offer the greatest potential for improved payment design.

4. The procedure allows for the detailed design of the pay packet structure in addition to the basic methods of payment.

5. The matching procedure draws attention to the assumptions of managerial practice in the design of payment systems and the rationale for certain shop floor working practices.

6. Finally, by relating the characteristics of the firms to their possible disruptive effect on the payment system, managerial authorities and decision-making processes might be more appropriately aligned and allocated — rather than assuming that the appointment of an industrial relations officer is sufficient in itself to cope with the firm's industrial relations problems.

### Assumptions, Values and Objectives of Payment

Management's values and assumptions about the utility of their payment methods in meeting their objectives are usually well protected. Not only are radical changes in payment methods rare and the full range of alternative payment methods rarely considered, but management assumptions about the design of payment methods frequently ignore the situational complexity to which they are applied. Consequently, many managers are unaware of some of their problems and unaware of the benefits that would come from changing their payment systems — because of their limited knowledge of alternatives and their uncritical acceptance of their current payment systems. The scepticism some managers expressed that the Lupton-Gowler procedure was academic (i.e. theoretical rather than practical) appeared to stem from their rejection of the suggestion in the book that alternative methods of payment were possible. Some managers did not consider certain alternative payment methods possible under any circumstances. Similarly there are those who would claim that the adoption of one particular method of payment would always achieve certain objectives. For example, Currie[13] claims that incentives decrease the direct need for supervision, improve methods of work, reduce absenteeism, and labour turnover. Brown[14] has advocated the incentives be abandoned as they stimulate envy and greed, and are a poor substitute for good management organisation. Yet others such as North and Buckingham[15] claim to have derived from 'model principles' three main elements that should make up a pay packet. The accounts given in this text do not unilaterally support any one of these positions. They stress particularly that changes in the payment rules or pay packet structure may not in themselves be sufficient to meet management objectives, or neatly resolve their immediate problems.

The objectives stated by management illustrate that some firms expect a great deal from their payment system whereas others expect little. The range of objectives included:

- retaining their labour force
- obtaining consistency in labour performance
- increasing output
- reducing rising labour costs and disputes
- improving product quality
- improving delivery times
- improving equipment utilisation
- obtaining a lower level of rejects
- reducing the level of 'work-in-progress'
- gaining control over the pay structure to reduce 'wage drift' and 'differential issues'

[13] *Financial Incentives*, B.I.M., 1965
[14] *Piecework Abandoned*, Heinemann, London, 1962.
[15] *Productivity Agreements And Wage Systems*, Gower Press, London 1969

— improving costing, methods, planning, work loading and labour flexibility.

In most cases the firms were pursuing specified objectives, but it is not necessary to assume that unless one has objectives the analysis is not useful. Analysis might reveal characteristics that suggest that management might usefully act in the situation if there is potential for improvement; certainly the analysis did lead firms to reformulate some of their objectives, particularly that of assuming that 'operative effort' alone was sufficient to meet their objectives. Obviously the importance of payment, the cost of labour or its operational significance will vary from firm to firm and consequently firms' objectives differ. Lupton and Gowler suggest that the appraisal of objectives should take account of the difference between:

(a) the situation profile as it currently is, *and*
(b) as it might be if management objectives on certain matters are realised, *or*
(c) as it might be if certain factors outside the control of management change.

In this manner management can assess the cost of changing or not changing their objectives in their particular circumstances, in the same manner as they might assess the cost of adhering to certain values and assumptions about payment. The potential for change might then include a change in management's own objectives and priorities (which would consequently influence the situational characteristics of the firm). For example, management might decide that priority be given to reducing delivery dates rather than controlling production costs — the changed production situation would then influence payment 'fit'.

A review of management's current and future objectives and their expected results should be included (Figure 31) in reviewing the payment system. A firm's objectives might be found to be incompatible.

As the objectives of payment and the dimensions that

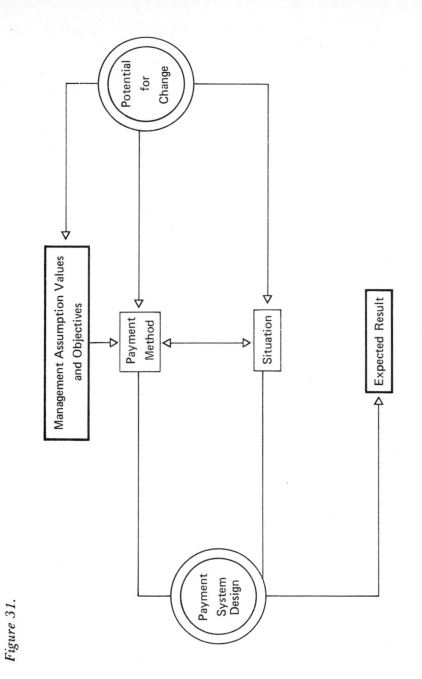

*Figure 31.*

123

influence it are diverse, a thorough assessment of a firm's payment system should consequently involve a mix of expertise. Too often it appears that it is those with certain professional backgrounds who foster their preferences in payment methods on to others, e.g. industrial engineers and work study practioners emphasize labour performance and focus on 'effort', whereas some personnel managers tend to favour a simple and stable wage structure and focus on 'reward'. In the firms examined in this book the evaluation of the payment system was undertaken in one firm as a project by an inter-specialist group, in some it was left to the personnel manager or work study specialist and in others it was undertaken as part of a manager's job. The piecemeal manner in which a payment system is used (and evaluated) is usually reflected in the fragmented procedures and information that bombard first line management. Information is usually supplied to and received from work study, cost, and personnel departments. Often these bits of information bear no obvious relation to each other. Such fragmentation of control may have its benefits, but rarely is the inter-relation between these procedures and reports appreciated. A frank review of the existing payment system by a number of different specialists might bring to light the fact that it is, for example, *not* designed to serve the managers responsible for departmental performance, or that it is merely a technical control, a numerical ritual or serves to provide information for limited decision-making e.g. the calculation of wages — if at all!

Weaknesses in payment are often attributed to their 'poor administration', and attempts to remedy this usually seek to secure support from senior management for the work study department or increase the staff of the department or improve control of the payment system on the shop-floor. However, if the further enforced administrative rationality does not 'fit' the requirements of the situation, operatives, supervisors and local managers would probably attempt to 'bend the rules' to overcome its malfunctioning. But if these attempts are unsuccessful and the administrative rationality is rigidly enforced, production might be disrupted, pay disputes occur, and labour turnover and absenteeism increase. The administrative application of a payment method to all of a firm's production areas, regardless of the diversity of circumstances or objectives within the firm, is frequently less than satisfactory. The consequent difficulty of ensuring that payment methods achieve their objectives and that equitable earnings and equitable efforts are maintained both within incentive areas and between incentive and non-incentive areas, might indicate the situational complexity underlying the generalised application of payment rules. The high cost of maintaining schemes, resistance to change, incidence of disputes, restriction of output and a loss of supervisory control might all be associated with 'misfit' situational characteristics. A firm may then be forced into managing its payment system by accepting overmanning and accepting low levels of output in areas of the firm in order to control 'parity' and 'differential' disputes within the firm. Others may resort to managing their payment system by constantly tightening slack 'work values' in order to maintain control over earnings levels — rather than examine and improve the situation that gives rise to 'slack values'. Others might qualify their payment system with so many allowances, additional rules and exceptions that management has built in to make it 'work' that its initial description may not bear out what it really is! The consequent 'blanket' administrative adjustments to a payment system that had previously been managed by such piecemeal adaption might be expected to meet with mixed if not chaotic results. Often such radical changes in payment methods are advocated with little or no attempt by management to readjust their situation. A firm might then change from an incentive payment method to measured day work to reduce 'bonus drift' and stabilise their wage structure only to find that they might still be experiencing a continuing increase in labour costs via 'grade drift', as management had not dealt with the numerous underlying and significant 'eroding' factors in their situation.

After management has completed a profile analysis of its production areas it might change radically from its usual administrative practices in managing the payment system. The management or improvement of the payment system may now be seen not to require a radical change in payment methods. Certain piecemeal situational changes might be seen to have a more significant impact. For example, following profile situational analysis management might consider that the payment system could be made more effective by changing or improving —

stock levels
technical services and process control
quality standards
material movement
equipment design
plant layout
production engineering activities.
production development activities
recruitment policy
maintenance procedures; machine reliability
investment decision on new plant
batch sizes
supervisory skills
raw materials
sub-contract work
product range and design
manning levels
market strategy
disputes, procedures and agreements
Or examining and reassessing —
basic payment, minimum earnings, guarantees
bonus payment
overtime payment, variations in hours worked
allowances paid
shift supplements
rules on changes in methods of payment
consolidation v fragmentation of payment
payment of supervision and management, supporting wage and salary structure
fringe benefits.

A firm's investment in improving its industrial relations

might then take the form of improving the situational 'fit' with its current payment method, or investing in improving the managerial and supervisory organisation in managing the 'misfit' dimensions of the situation in addition to examining the implications of restructuring the firm's payment methods. The strategy for improvement adopted may not necessarily be a 'pure' strategy for dealing with labour market difficulties or dispute procedures, or for dealing solely with certain of the technological dimensions. Because many of the profile dimensions are interrelated a 'mixed' or 'offset' strategy might be appropriate. In some parts of the firm the labour force might need to be stabilised, whereas in others maintainance procedures or stock levels may need to be adjusted. An 'offset' strategy might include improving labour skill and flexibility in order to combat technological difficulties rather than improving technological characteristics and employing a less skilled labour force. One might decide to improve supervisory skill to cope with innovations rather than restricting innovation and reducing supervisory costs. These types of strategies might prove to be a useful way of managing the payment system.

Attempts to reduce labour costs by reducing wage demands or stabilising the wage structure of a firm appear to be best examined by reviewing payment methods in their particular work context. In some circumstances adjustments or changes might increase unit costs and limit management's own flexibility and in others there might be scope for improved productivity. The profile method of analysis indicates how far the firm is managing its payment system in relation to product and technological innovation, labour market constraints, and other structural factors. It also makes firms aware of the impact of having research and development activity in the production area, the impact of rationalisation or diversification and the effect of sub-contracting certain operations or products or of changing its stock policy. Although appraising the payment system might well be part of management's objective of improving their labour relations and reducing strikes and disputes, reappraisal also seems necessary when increasing the level of automation or reorganising production and so on.

127

Comparing the Lupton-Gowler method with the other procedures adopted to select or diagnose faults in payment, one finds that most of the firms ignored many of the dimensions of the situation and tended to concentrate on the abstract nature of the pay rules. Some firms had used consultants who were primarily concerned to have their 'package' recommendations accepted by management. Other firms had felt uneasy about their payment systems because larger firms were changing to other payment methods. Yet others had assumed that mere managerial consensus on the payment system was sufficient to improve the system. Although managerial commitment and backing is important to a payment system, if the system is inappropriate such support would only waste resources. In several firms it was obvious that the traditional payment method would be reapplied solely because it had been a success in the past and nobody knew of any other alternative. The more calculative approach of undertaking an earning audit i.e. analysing the earnings structure, the movement of earnings over periods of time and between different sites, was more useful, though attention was primarily focused on the 'reward' structure i.e. the analysis of individual pay packets and the wage structure. No attention was given to the situational dimensions that had and might still disrupt, the relation between 'effort' and 'reward', and so influence the firm's productivity. The Lupton-Gowler method introduces a wider range of dimensions that managers should consider and stresses the inter-relationships between the various dimensions. By stressing the underlying forces of a payment situation, their method has given the analysis of payment systems a completely new perspective and a more positive guide to the improvement of payment design.

The rationale for changing or maintaining a particular method of payment might then be based on an evaluation of the implications and costs of different payment methods and an assessment of their suitability to a firm's circumstances and objectives; rather than being based on statements of belief or conviction about whether one could 'trust people', 'treat them as responsible human beings' or on the assertion that some methods are 'old-fashioned'. The positions that some managers take up in discussing the advantages and disadvantages of different payment methods, the best procedures for establishing 'standards' and the advantages and disadvantages of centralising or decentralising the control of the payment system, appear to be relatively meaningless unless reference is made to a particular situation. Similarly, the current emphasis put on disputes and dispute procedures *appears* to be a relatively insignificant aspect of the typical payment situation compared with some of its other characteristics.

The Lupton-Gowler framework of analysis is useful in developing a labour strategy as an integral part of a firm's objectives and circumstances, as it is able to take account of the unique aspects of certain areas of a firm, as well as the more general aspects that might prevade all of the profiled areas of the firm. Improved wage payment design and the management of payment system should follow its application.

# 5     Some Technical Points

In this section some points are made that might assist profile scoring and interpretation.

The method of profiling rests on management's definition of the situation, and consequently if management are ill-informed or complete the procedure in a superficial mannner, the result would be misleading. As with any other procedure the Lupton-Gowler procedure can be well or badly used.

The completion of profiling within a firm should rapidly bring to light the dimensions that cause difficulty in managing the payment system. The examination of 'misfit' dimensions and an appreciation of how far they are typical of the firm's situation should be carefully assessed. The first question that might be asked of each dimension are — what is the current effect of having the recorded 'misfit' dimension? Which 'misfit' dimensions are highly sensitive to increasing output, increasing costs, represent constraints or are the main dimensions that had disrupted the payment system in the past? Should operator 'effort' be directed solely towards dealing with a few misfit dimensions, or would supervisory and managerial 'efforts' be more effective?

As the scoring of the dimensions is based on a six monthly period, note should be taken of how typical this six monthly period is or how far the future pattern would be the same. For example, in several firms the characteristics of the technology and product market currently required periodic and significant recruitment and redundancy over cycles of years. This would obviously influence the profile dimensions associated with the characteristics of the labour force — for example if the firm has a 'last in, first out' policy the age structure of the firm might change radically, influencing training, absence and so on. Redundancy procedures and agreements might be reviewed critically in the light of their effect on the payment system.

Though managers sometimes work with a number of the situational dimensions identified by Lupton and Gowler, they rarely look at all of the profile dimensions and in particular often do not examine the inter-relationships between the profile dimensions. These 'linkages' are important in considering the implications for change and draw attention to the fact that there is often more than one way to solve a payment system problem. It is not possible to state what the relationships will be and how significant they might be in the areas analysed. This can only be discovered by examining the 'dynamic' in the particular areas analysed.

In the light of its application in other firms *a simplified checklist of the steps that were taken* within a firm were:

1. Select areas of analysis
2. Decide the appropriate level of analysis
3. Examine the current implications of the payment situation — both in terms of the pay packet structure and behaviour, 'custom and practice' of operatives, supervision and management.
4. Examine the scope for improved 'effort' by operatives, supervision and management.
5. Evaluate in terms of costs, constraints, and management's values and objectives.
6. Devise a strategy for change (or the avoidance of change) by redesigning the situation and/or payment rules.

In relation to steps 5 and 6 the profile analysis of several areas within a firm might necessitate the evaluation of the following alternative short-term and long-term strategies:

(a) adopting the payment method that 'fits' *most* of the areas throughout the firm
(b) adopting the payment method that best 'fits' those areas of the firm that management regards as *critical*

(c) adopting different payment methods that are best fitted for each area
(d) remaining with the current payment methods but making (if possible) adjustments to aspects of the situation to improve the 'fit'
(e) assessing the potential for situational and payment rule changes and developing a strategy for managing *both* as an integral way of improving productivity within the firm.

Alternatively, management might use the profile analysis of various areas within a firm as a basis for further discussion with supervision and management or require the completion of a report on the possibilities of improvement within each 'area'. In this manner a firm's strategy for managing its payment system might consist of improving its quality control or changing the design of its products in some areas; whereas in other areas adjustment might be made to the structure of the pay packet by recognising that current circumstances now require the provision of 'allowances' and so on. Equitable earnings and 'efforts' might then be managed in this piecemeal manner as they might also be affected by a radical change in the firm's payment methods.

The profile dimensions are now commented on to elaborate on some of the problems of definition that arose, and the implications for certain dimensional scores and changes in scores (movement of dimensions).

## Effort and Accountability

One weakness in the original Lupton-Gowler text was the insufficient guidance given on how to select the areas and the appropriate level of analysis at which the method should be applied. No clear-cut rules were given on this, even though it has significant implications for the firm's administrative bargaining structure once the types of 'effort' and basis of accountability have been formally recognised. A firm's resultant pay structure and its movement is shaped by these decisions in addition to the situational characteristics of the firm.

## 1(g) Type of Effort

It is suggested that the major distinction in payment methods be made between 'energy' and 'time/competence' schemes. The basic choice should now be represented as:

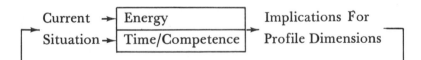

## 2(g) Unit of Accountability

As an indication of the importance of reassessing this in designing the payment system, the reader is referred to the example of the Misto Plant:

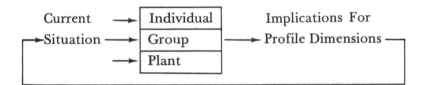

## 1. Length of the Job Cycle

This was defined as the average for those employees in the area analysed. Discussion of 'the job' was useful as it would establish exactly what was included or excluded. The nature of 'the job' might also affect the composition of the labour force by requiring the type of physical or mental characteristics typical of a certain age-sex group — which in itself might present difficulties in the local labour market. In those firms that paid by the hour the job cycle might be less clearly defined than in those firms that used work measurement to determine the job. The job cycle might also give clues to other aspects of the profile — for example, a long job cycle might suggest that a long period of training is required, part of dimension (10); the cost of time-study might be high: if it is difficult to define, this might suggest that the labour force is very flexible and so on. The length of the job cycle might vary with the rate of product change, or be associated with the incidence of job stoppages.

## 2. Number of Job Modifications

Here it was important to distinguish (or at least not to double score) job modifications and product changes. The magnitude of this dimension was probably greater that is often recognised by management.

## 3. Degree of Automation

When scoring this dimension, a frequent problem was that the area being analysed might contain a "mix" of machinery. This might suggest that the basis of the proposed scheme should be changed to take account of such differences. An analysis was undertaken in one machine shop[16] which demonstrated that there were significant profile differences between the different types of machinery (i.e. job cycle, modifications, product change and the pattern of stoppages). It is recommended that all of the mix is scored and the implications of the different technology assessed in its relation to the other dimensions of the situation. In practice it appears that the highest scoring degree of automation recorded has the most dominating influence on a profiled situation. Certain advanced production line complexes were often similar to the most complex degree of automation. Plant behaviour might well change over its life cycle and consequently this might also influence the payment system.

## 4. Product Change

This does not necessarily refer to the final product, e.g. a

[16] This point is illustrated in one of the collection of three additional case studies available from the author.

machine shop may have a high rate of product change if it is dealing with a large number of product lines and contracted work — whereas the final assembly shop may have a very low rate of product change. As with labour, machinery might also be acquired to make a specific product — this might substantially reduce the rate of product change. The rate of product change score would be influenced by changes in product design, standardising parts, changing the product range, stock levels or re-routing work. An analysis of the impact of product innovation, or the product life cycle, on the payment system might be useful if not essential to understanding earnings movements in some firms.

## 5. & 6. The Number and Duration of Job Stoppages

These scores usually referred to the average for the individual in the area analysed. These two dimensions are primarily influenced by a time-saved incentive: the most common form of incentive. Changes in the incidence of stoppages beyond the control of the operative might influence the level of earnings (output) and disputes over 'rates' for stoppages. An examination of stoppages might reveal the possibility of reducing them by improving "indirect" services, supervision and plant technology rather than, for example, introducing an incentive scheme.

## 7. Percentage of Job Elements Specified

Although the scores obtained on this dimension were usually recorded as 71 per cent and over, it seems that the high specification given in some areas was optimistic. The situational requirements that necessitate operative skill and flexibility might also make this a 'misfit' dimension.

## 8. & 9. Percentage of Material Scrapped and Rejected

As with the dimensions of product change and job

modifications, it is important to clarify this and not double score. Levels of scrap and rejects might be influenced by different materials, changes in technology, batch size or training periods. Material utilisation incentives were often used when material costs were a high proportion of total costs (and often other misfit dimensions were ignored in the design of such incentives).

### 10. Time Required to Fill a Vacancy

Some firms' labour market conditions were such that they could obtain a fully-trained man at a few days notice; in others the labour market, if not the training or re-training period, weakened the method of payment. Several firms maintained a buffer of labour, either in the form of a formal or informal labour pool.

### 11. & 12. Labour Stability and Labour Turnover

The operation of these two dimensions over time determines the composition of the labour force. The characteristics of the firm's technology, product and labour market, as well as management-union agreements on earnings guarantees, job security, recruitment, retention, re-deployment, redundancy and retirement, shape the labour force. Its composition would also have implications for the training and re-training of the labour force within the firm.

### 13. & 14. Disputes about Pay (Number and Duration)

In spite of the fact that the examples of profile analysis concentrated on cases of 'pathological' payment systems, disputes about pay did not appear to be significant — adjustment to the payment system took other forms.

## 15. Percentage of Earnings Decided Outside the Plant or Company

A major factor that might limit the selection of the method of payment may be the constraints of national agreements which might determine basic, bonus or premium rates. This structure of agreed rates may facilitate or constrain local management in its objectives. Some firms analysed their particular situation in terms of their national agreements — in part they were attempting to change the situational factors to improve their 'fit' to such fixed agreements on payment, and did not consider alternative domestic agreements for part or all of their factory. Other firms selectively ignored certain national provisions and yet others had opted out of being influenced by such agreements and procedures at all.


## 16. Number of Trade Unions

On this dimension the importance of mergers or splits of unions and increasing unionisation within a firm would influence the payment system. The payment system would need to be designed so as to maintain or restore differentials and cope with the national and domestic agreements of the various unions.


## 17. Occupational Structure.

The complexity of the occupational structure that might be required by the technology, product market characteristics and union demands might create a 'leap-frog' differential bargaining structure.


## 18. Absence

Might be associated with the composition of the labour force (age and sex structure), technology and so on. This would affect the payment system by the need to overcome these labour shortages by redeployment or over-manning. Some firms have introduced incentive payments to reduce absence and others have attempted to control such disruptive consequences on production by making agreed absence (time-off) part of the reward structure.

## 19. & 21. Average Age of Working Force and Percentage of Males in the Work Force.

An analysis of the structure and composition of the labour force would reveal how significant these characteristics are in influencing the effectiveness of the payment system[17] .  .

## 20. Percentage Labour Cost in Unit Cost.

The proportion of labour costs is a significant factor in determining how important labour utilisation is in the particular area analysed. From profile analysis it should be apparent that managers can exercise some choice on whether labour costs might be higher or lower, if they are willing to examine the costs and benefits of alternative situational change to the payment system.

## New Dimension —

## 22. Raw Material Variation[18]

Although this dimension is often related to dimensions (8) & (9) it is also useful to score this particular dimension in the production situation. A suggested scaling on the profile is one to fifteen percent. If this factor is shown to be a significant 'eroding' factor, management might consider improving

[17] For a detailed account of the effect of the changing composition of the labour force (via labour turnover) on productivity see Karen Legge *The Operation of the 'Regressive Spiral' in the Labour Market* Journal of Management Studies Vol.7 No.1. February 1970.
[18] Identified in a detailed study by Cecily Gorfin.

quality control, changing raw materials or, as is sometimes the case, improving control of the technology which produces or processes the 'raw' material.

These specific dimensions provide a useful framework for examining a firm's payment system. The application of the procedure should provide managers with useful 'insights' into the dynamics of their own situations. Not only does the procedure indicate where 'operative efforts' might be usefully directed towards increasing productivity, but it also indicates the scope for productivity improvements that might be effected via 'supervisory and managerial efforts'. Management strategies for productivity and payment design improvement should consider both (Figure 32).

Many managers attempt to deal with their 'human and industrial relations' with little awareness of the characteristics of the structures within their firm. Managerial good intent by itself is often insufficient to cope with the complexity and dynamic of the situations they are attempting to manage. Even in those firms where apparently 'good industrial relations practice' is rampant, for example, where elaborate communication and consultative procedures exist and recognition is given to the rights of employees and trade unions, the Lupton-Gowler framework of analysis unfortunately illustrates that satisfactory human and industrial relations are not then adequately safeguarded by such procedures and practices alone. 'Standards' and patterns of behaviour are influenced by other forces in the work situation, not solely by agreed rules and procedures. However, it would appear that there is some scope for avoiding the avoidable 'human and industrial problems' by improved payment system design with this method and ideas.

If the reader requires further and more detailed examples of the uses of this method a collection of three additional case studies are available from the author. These might be particularly useful for educational and training purposes.

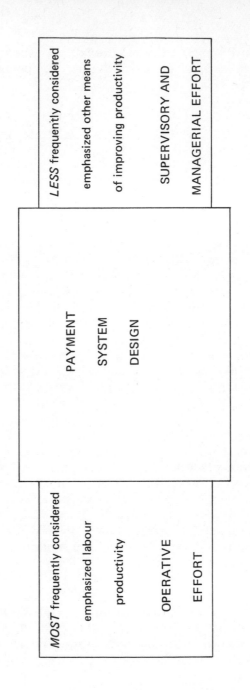

*Figure 32. Management Strategies for Productivity Improvement.*

# Appendix
# Profile dimensions-notes on scoring

Before scoring each dimension decide which unit of production is being considered;* an individual, a section, a workshop, a department, a plant, a company, and score consistently for that unit. It may be found necessary, or useful, to construct profiles for each department, so that similarities and differences are clearly shown up. The comparison will indicate whether one, or a number of payment schemes is appropriate. It is also possible to derive from a number of profiles that effort/reward relationship which is common to each of the units considered.

### 'Gate' mechanism

*Type of effort 1(g).* It is necessary to identify the type of effort appropriate to the unit concerned, thus:

(a) establish whether the work is skilled or professional. If it is score C for competence effort. If it is not competence effort then move to
(b) and establish whether the effort is intensive, i.e., output effort measured against some predetermined standard. If it is then score E for energy effort. If not then move to
(c) and score T for time effort, i.e. pay for the hour by the hour.

*Unit of accountability 2(g). Individual accountability*

* The 'score' on the Unit of Accountability dimensions dictates whether individual group or plant reward in the Master Block should be picked up by the situation profile.

141

means that the work of an individual can be clearly distinguished. *Group accountability* is scored when the contribution of the individual to the co-operative task of a small group (i.e. under 20 persons but more than one) is impossible, or difficult to distinguish (or is thought undesirable to distinguish). Plant accountability is scored when the contribution of the individual or a small group to the task being carried out by a large group (20+) is impossible, or difficult to distinguish (or is thought undesirable to distinguish).

## Profile dimensions

*Length of job cycle.* The time it takes to complete the sequence of operations that comprise what is defined or usually recognized as the job.** Scale from 0-121 minutes.

*Number of job modifications.* Take each job done during the period (say six months) and record the number of times the instructions for doing the job (as defined in 1 above) have been formally changed, i.e. have been written down. Scale from 0-8+ per month.

*Degree of automation.* The categories along the dimension are:

SPT: single purpose hand tools, e.g. handsaw, hammer and chisel.

PAT: single purpose power-driven hand tools, e.g. pneumatic drill.

SMT: simple machine tools, e.g. centre lathe, shaper, radial arm driller, circular saw.

CMT: complex machine tools, e.g. gear cutting machines.

STM: simple transfer machines, i.e. automatic sequence of

** Where there are a number of jobs involved average job-cycle times and modifications should be calculated.

142

similar operations e.g. drilling and facing.

CTM: complex transfer machines, embodying automatic sequences of dissimilar operations.

SPO: simple process operations e.g. rolling mill and blast-furnace operations.

CPO: complex process operations, e.g. instrument controlled chemical process.

CCP: continuous complex process operations, e.g. a chemical process with on-line computer control.

*Product changes.* We define a product change as either the introduction of a completely new product into the range, or a change-over in a production unit from one product to another, both of which are already in the firm's present range. Scale from 0-8+ changes per month. (For example, in a garment factory an order for 500 dresses of a new fashion, or a re-order of a conventional garment would both be product changes. In a jobbing engineering firm every new order or repeat order is a product change).

*Job stoppages (number)* Record the average daily occasions when work was stopped. Scale 0-8+ stoppages per day — for such reasons as:

(a) shortage of materials
(b) shortage of components
(c) poor quality materials
(d) shortage of tools
(e) absence of service
(f) shortage of labour
(g) absence of instructions
(h) ambiguous instructions
(i) machine/process failure

*Job stoppages duration.* The duration in minutes of job stoppages, as defined in 5, above. Scale 0-61+ minutes

143

(average per day).

*Percentage of job elements specified by management.* State (on average) what percentage of the elements of each job is not at the discretion of the worker but is:

    (a) prescribed by management, and/or
    (b) controlled by machine
Scale +71% − 0%

*Percentage material scrapped.* Sum all materials put into production/service each day and average for the period concerned how much has been recorded as wasted, i.e.

    (a) has been spoiled by (i) poor workmanship, (ii) poor tools and (iii) poor organization, and
    (b) has been scrapped necessarily in production (e.g. material lost by cutting and machining).
Scale 0% − 15% + average daily wastage.

*Percentage product/components scrapped.* Record the percentage of all components and finished products, put into production/service each day, that were rejected as substandard (this differs from 8 in being concerned with what happens at points where work is checked for quality). Scale 0% − 15% + average rejects daily.

*Time required to fill a vacancy.* Record for the period concerned the average time elapsed from the notification of a vacancy to the filling of a vacancy by a person competent to do the job.

*Labour stability.* The labour stability index (devised by Angela Bowey) is arrived at by the following formula:

$$\frac{Ln}{n \times N} \times 100$$

N is the total number of employees,
n is the number of months over which stability is being measured,

Ln is the total length of service in months of the employees concerned measured over the past n months.

This formula expresses stability as a percentage of the maximum possible stability.

Labour stability measures the ability of the unit to retain its employees, as distinct from labour turnover which measures the rate of replacement of employees. The significant difference between these two measures is illustrated, for instance, where a high labour turnover rate is due mostly to a small proportion of jobs in the unit being filled several times in the time period considered. High labour turnover in this example does not indicate low labour stability. Scale +81% − 0%

*Labour turnover.* This is measured by the usual formula, i.e.

$$\frac{\text{total no. leavers x } 100}{\text{average no. employed during period}}$$

However, it must be noted that leavers here includes all those transferred to another unit of production.

Scale 0% - 48% + men
     0% - 96% + women

*Disputes about pay (number).* State how many disputes were recorded each month during the period concerned which were about the amount of pay. For example, a claim for a money allowance for some special circumstances, which is not admitted by management, is a dispute, so is a refusal of an operator to be transferred on the grounds that his bonus earnings would suffer, and so is a refusal to accept regrading. If no detailed records are kept, a 'straw-poll' of supervisors, shop-stewards and work study men, might suffice to produce a figure for a typical month. Scale 0 − 33+ disputes (average) per month.

*Disputes about pay (duration).* Record total hours lost through pay disputes as defined in 13 above, and express these as a percentage of total normal hours. Scale 0% − 33%+

*Percentage earnings decided outside plant/company.* Take the average total earnings of the workers in the unit under consideration and state what percentage is the outcome of settlement made outside the firm, e.g. by a employers' federation and a union confederation nationally, or by statute. Scale 0% — 81% +

*Number of Trade Unions.* This refers to the number of trade unions in the whole plant/company under consideration whose representatives bargain with management representatives. Scale 0 — 22 +

*Occupational structure.* Multiply the total number of grades in the plant/company by the total number of administrative units, by the number of shifts worked to arrive at a measure of the complexity of occupational structure.

$$\frac{\text{grades x number of admin. units x number of shifts}}{100}$$

For example: if a job evaluated grading structure has 4 grades, and there are some 100 administrative units*** in the plant/company, and 2 shifts are worked we have

$$\frac{4 \times 100 \times 2}{100} = 8$$

This is intended as a measure of the potentiality of earnings movements to 'leap-frog'. Scale 0 - 25 +

*Percentage absence.* Recorded absence from the unit *for any reason,* including time lost through strikes, sickness, absence, days off, and lateness are included, but not lay-offs due to e.g., shortage of materials, or managerial shortcomings. Scale 0% — 16% +

*Average age of work force.* Three point scale i.e. 15-29 years, 30-44 years and 45+ years.

*Percentage labour cost in product cost.* Percentage of direct labour cost in the total production costs generated by

*** The number of units administered by first line management.

146

the unit concerned.

*Percentage males in working force* (all plant/company). This is obvious. Scale 0% — 71% +

*Note on the time period.* Lupton and Gowler suggest that the data needed for the completion of a situation profile should be collected over at least six months previous to the exercise. The scales have been constructed with this time period in mind, but care should be taken to allow for seasonal fluctuations that might occur outside the period selected for data collection.

# Index